Vintage
Electric Guitars

In Praise of
Fretted Americana

Photography by Bill Ingalls Jr.
Text by Willie G. Moseley
Foreword by Jeff Carlisi

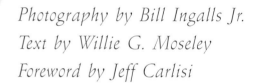

4880 Lower Valley Road, Atglen, PA 19310 USA

Designed by John P. Cheek
Type set in Huxley Vertical BT/Souvenir Lt BT

ISBN: 0-7643-1361-4
Printed in China
1 2 3 4

Published by Schiffer Publishing Ltd.
4880 Lower Valley Road
Atglen, PA 19310
Phone: (610) 593-1777; Fax: (610) 593-2002
E-mail: Schifferbk@aol.com
Please visit our web site catalog at
www.schifferbooks.com or write for a free catalog.

We are always looking for authors to write books on
new and related subjects. If you have an idea for a
book, please contact us at the above address.

This book may be purchased from the publisher.
Please include $3.95 for shipping.

In Europe, Schiffer books are distributed by
Bushwood Books
6 Marksbury Ave.
Kew Gardens
Surrey TW9 4JF England
Phone: 44 (0)20-8392-8585;
Fax: 44 (0)20-8392-9876
E-mail: Bushwd@aol.com
Free postage in the UK. Europe: Air mail at cost.
Please try your bookstore first.

Vintage Electric Guitars

CONTENTS

ACKNOWLEDGMENTS

Bill Ingalls Jr. would like to thank Margaret, Bill Sr., Judy, and Willie.

Willie G. Moseley would like to thank Gail and Elizabeth, Cleo and Alan and their associates at Vintage Guitar, Inc., Arnold, Dimitri, Barney, and Bill Jr. (and a special "read-between-the-lines" salute to the Messrs. Spilman for encouraging me to become a full-time writer).

Special thanks for additional input and information: Paul Bechtoldt, Walter Carter, Mike Newton, Steve Soest, Tom Wittrock, Michael Wright

Most of all, thanks for the guitars: Rudy Abbott, Tommy Allen, Clay Bailey, Paul Bailey Jr., Jerry Baker, Lyle and Jim Ball, Hansel Bateman, Rodney Bateman, Henry Batton, Wes Bentley, Craig Boehme, Greg Bozeman, Larry Briggs, John Brinkmann, Sharon Bryant, Luke Burdett, Eddie Campbell, Jeff Carlisi, Bill Chain, Steve Cherne, Chip Coleman, James Cooksey, Bill Covington, Lamar Crawford, Dave Crocker, Dave Davis, Jim DeStafney, Michael Dickens, Doug Dickerson, Charles Dyess, Andy Eder, Barry Ehrlich, T.C. Eldridge, Tim Evans, "Bear" Faulkner, W.D. Faulkner, Arnold Finkelstein, Steve Fjestad, Terry Franklin, Hobbie Freehling, Charles Garris, Steve Garris, Joe Gilchrist, Jack Goodson, Muryl Grant, Gary Grubbs, Jamie Hamilton, Thomas Hand, Mark Hayes, Gregg Hopkins, Charles Hubbard, Darrell Huff, Mark Hughes, Doug Jackson, Bill Johnson, Melissa Jones, Bill Kaman, Howard Keel, Rick King, Ken Kirkland, John Kotlowski, Philip Leitz, Rick Lowell, Ronnie Lowell, James Madden, Roy Majors, Steve Maness, Mike "Chainsaw" McCullough, Shannon McPherson, Dick Merritt, Johnny Milteer, Newman Milteer, Don Murdoch, Chris Narmour, John Nelson, Dave Newman, Nick Nicholas, Mark Pace, Daryl Payton, Derrick Paoletto, Kerry Patterson, Jick Pendergraft, Harry Perkins, Jay Pilzer, "Doc" Petillo, Carl Ponder, Steve Powell, Dean Powers, David Rines, Barney Roach, Duck Robinson, Dave Rogers, Jay Rosen, Marty Ruckel, Grady Sanders, Don Schwartz, Ed Seelig, Don Sheehan, Steve Soest, Gil Southworth, Bill Spivey, Ken Spivey, Randy Spivey, Vince Swanson, Frank Tanton, Mike Vague, Peter Vitale, Bobby Walker, Bill Whatley, Mark Willis, Tommy Willis, Richard Lee Young.

FOREWORD

Most of us can remember exactly where we were during the certain events (we might even remember the aroma of Mom's food cooking on the stove). For me, one of those lifelong memories was when I was sitting on the floor in the den at my parents' house in Jacksonville, Florida. On that particular Sunday night in 1964, I watched the Beatles' first appearance on *The Ed Sullivan Show*. For many kids, there was the fascination with the screaming fans, the look of the lads, and of course, the trademark "*wooos*," compliments of Little Richard. I must say, however, that for me it was more the look, the sound, and the mystique of those electric guitars. How cool!

From that moment on, I understood the true meaning of the word *passion*, and like most of us, I headed straight to the Sears catalog to have a look. It seems strange now that Sears took precedent over the local music store, which probably carried Gretsch and Rickenbacker, not to mention a few leftover sunburst Les Pauls. We all remember those Danelectro-made Silvertones in their novel and handy amplifier cases, but for me, it was that triple-pickup, Harmony-made model with all the switches (wouldn't you know I'd pick the most expensive one). Man, I never got tired of staring at that page!

My first guitar *was* a Silvertone, albeit a $10 acoustic (and I still have it). I played that thing for two years, and had I known anything about "string action" back then, I would have taken up Dobro! Needless to say, my fingers were very happy when my dad bought me my first electric guitar, a double-pickup Gibson Melody Maker in a sunburst finish. Now I was cool, and that guitar only helped fuel the passion I had for the instrument—it truly was a guitar for "Everyman." Throughout the years, and like so many others, I owned various guitars. Keep in mind that in the "pre-vintage era," we bought guitars based not only on our proficiency as musicians, but also our financial situation (including how much dough Mom and Dad were willing to shell out). To this day, I believe that a lot of up-and-coming rockers in the '60s were given the opportunity to develop their talents simply because there were so many "egalitarian" guitars out there that everyone could afford.

My next guitar was a "reverse" Firebird III. When I saw Keith Richards and Brian Jones playing identical Firebird VIIs on—where else—*The Ed Sullivan Show*, I knew I had to have one. By today's standard, mind you, a 1964 Firebird III might not be considered "egalitarian," but in those days it was both available and affordable.

Does anyone remember the film footage of Cream performing "Crossroads," where Eric Clapton's playing a normal Firebird I? Who can forget the humongous tone that Mountain's Leslie West milked out of his Les Paul Jr.? These guitars and others like them played a major role in shaping the sound of contemporary music. I have to say that it seems somewhat ironic, considering the vintage hype of the last several years, how manufacturers such as Gibson and Fender are re-issuing examples of their Holy Grails, with other companies following suit. Alleluia!

Throughout Bill and Willie's book, you will find many examples of "egalitarian" guitars, but you'll also see one-offs and bizarre rarities. No longer will these unique instruments be relegated to the back seat of notoriety, thanks to Bill's camera and Willie's typewriter. They all have their place in the evolutionary chain of six-string electric Spanish guitars, and may the manufacturers producing instruments for today's market continue to arouse the passion of every young (and not-so-young) "plank spanker" for years to come.

Hey Bill and Willie—wanna start a band?

Jeff Carlisi

LEXICON

As is the case with most collectibles, the vintage guitar phenomenon is replete with its own unique assortment of terms and acronyms. While many of them are associated with specific brands and/or models and will be noted in specific chapters (Valco's "Gumby"-shaped headstocks, Gibson's pioneering "semi-solid" ES-335), it's also helpful to be familiar with some basic construction features of electric guitars, particularly from an aesthetic point of view:

ACTIVE CIRCUITRY: Some instruments have solid-state circuitry built into them, which usually provides additional sonic options (volume boost, instant tone changes, compression, etc.). Such circuitry is usually powered by a 9-volt battery that is also installed in the instrument.

ARCH-TOP: Guitar with a curved (and sometimes carved) top, such as the Gibson ES-175. Most electric-acoustic arch-tops have two f-holes for a bit of acoustic reference, and some had fully-acoustic predecessors.

BINDING: Material (usually flexible plastic) that "binds" edges of wood together; however, sometimes binding has a strictly cosmetic usage.

BRIDGE: Part on top of guitar body where strings "transmit" vibrations to the body for sonic reproduction. A bridge usually has small grooves in it to accommodate each string, and is usually made of wood or metal. Most bridges on electric guitars allow adjustment of string height, and many bridges also allow better intonation/fine-tuning with individual adjustable saddles for each string, which can be moved forward or backward to change length of the vibrating part of a string (between bridge and nut).

CONTOUR: Beveling on solidbody instruments to enhance comfort, as pioneered by the Fender Stratocaster in the mid-'50s. A "belly cut" is found on

the back of an instrument and a "forearm bevel" is found on the top. Both of these individual contour terms are self-explanatory.

CUTAWAY: Portion of guitar near neck/body joint that has been "cut out" to allow access to higher frets on the neck, creating a "horn" on the body. Instruments may be single-cutaway (many Gibson instruments, Fender Telecaster), offset double-cutaway (Fender Stratocaster, Fender basses), or symmetrical double-cutaway (Gibson ES-335, Standel 510-S). Gibson's SG-style bodies look symmetrical at first glance, but are in fact slightly offset. Cutaways, if found on electric-acoustic instruments (usually archtops) are usually dubbed "Florentine" if the horn is pointed (Gibson ES-175) or "Venetian" if the horn is rounded (Gibson Byrdland—but some Byrdlands had Florentine cutaways).

F-HOLE: F-shaped soundhole (as seen on violins and other classical instruments), usually found on arch-top guitars.

FLAT-TOP: The classic *acoustic* guitar configuration; only a few electric examples will be encountered herein.

FRET: Each space on a guitar fingerboard/fretboard; serves the same function as a piano key by changing the pitch of a string by one note. The metal strips that delineate each fret are made of "fret wire," an alloy.

HEADSTOCK: Top of instrument where the tuning keys and brand name are (usually) found.

JACK: Receptacle for guitar cord.

NUT: Small grooved part between headstock and fretboard, usually made of bone, plastic, or metal. Some newer instruments have nuts made of space-age composite material.

that shields guitar body from pick damage; also known as a "scratchplate." Pickguards are usually mounted in an elevated position on brackets (as seen on most arch-top guitars) or flush on a guitar body (as seen on most solidbody and flat-top guitars).

PICKUP: Microphone-like device consisting of magnet(s) and wiring that "picks up" string vibrations. "Single-coil" pickups have a self-describing designation, while "humbucking" pickups have two coils, wired in opposition to each other to cancel out annoying electronic noise. While most pickups are mounted on a guitar body, some transducer-type pickups are built into a guitar's bridge (and usually aren't visible). Many pickups have individual "polepieces" (one for each string) for more efficient reception. Some polepieces are even threaded, and can be adjusted for height.

POSITION MARKERS: Also known as "fret markers;" simply decorative inlays (usually dots or blocks) noting certain frets for player reference.

POTENTIOMETERS: Potentiometers ("pots") aren't visible, but are critical in an electric guitar's overall makeup. Pots are the electronic controls under volume and tone knobs, and many of them have an Electronic Industries Association code stamped into them (if the pots were made in the U.S.) that notes their date of manufacture. If an instrument has no serial number (or a serial number has been intentionally removed), dating the potentiometers can assist in dating the instrument itself, if the pots are original.

SCALE: Distance from nut to bridge, usually standardized on most Gibson guitars (24¾ inches) and Fender guitars (25½ inches). Fender's 34-inch scale on their basses has pretty much become the industry standard, but some short-scale (30-30½ inches) basses will be encountered herein, as will a couple of medium-scale (32-inch) basses.

TAILPIECE: Anchor point for "ball end" of string. Independent tailpieces are usually "stop"-type (as seen on a lot of Gibsons) or "trapeze-type" (as seen on most arch-top electrics). Many times, the bridge and tailpiece are combined into one unit, and many times, that one unit also has a vibrato system built into it.

TOGGLE SWITCH: Turns individual pickups off and on. Obviously, this item wouldn't be found on a single-pickup guitar, and the Fender Esquire's switch that seems to be an incongruity is actually a tone switch.

TRUSS ROD COVER: Most guitars have a metal truss rod inside the neck, to help alleviate string tension (which could cause the neck to warp). The truss rod is usually adjustable, and on some brands such as Gibson and Guild, a small plate on the headstock covers the access point. In the case of many bolt-on necks, the truss rod can be adjusted by removing the neck.

VIBRATO: A device that allows a player to change the pitch of a string (or strings), evoking a modulating tone. A guitar vibrato usually utilizes springs mounted on the device itself (Bigsby) or inside the guitar body (Fender Stratocaster). Gibson's Vibrola is a dubious exception, as we'll soon see.

OTHER TERMS

HOUSE BRANDS: Private-label guitars and basses that were marketed by retailers such as Sears (Silvertone), or wholesale distributors such as St. Louis Music (Custom Kraft). American-made house brand instruments were usually made by budget guitar manufacturers such as Harmony, Kay, Valco and Danelectro, although Gibson and Rickenbacker have also made private label guitars during their respective histories.

NEW OLD STOCK ("N.O.S."): Indicates an instrument that may be decades old, but was never sold at retail, for one of several anomalous reasons. Ferreting out such oddities is one of the intriguing facets of the vintage guitar phenomenon.

"VINTAGE": Subject to debate concerning older guitars. Many persons use the 25-year mark to differentiate between "vintage" and simply "used". The instruments in this book that were made post-1975 are either discontinued models (except for one) or modern instruments that have a "retro-cool" vibe.

A WORD ABOUT PRICING

The prices in this book are estimated retail values for the instruments shown in the condition that you see. Wear, modifications, etc., can figure into the desirability (therefore price) of individual instruments, as can market trends or fads, so don't presume other examples of the models seen in this book could be bought or sold for these retail estimates. As clichéd as it may sound, "What it's worth is what someone's willing to sell it for, and what someone's willing to pay for it" – simple as that.

"Bursts"? Been there, done that. Custom-color Fenders? Check, please. Original '50s korina-bodied, "modernistic"...aw, you get the idea.

While encountering a highly-desirable, classic example of fretted Americana (electric *or* acoustic) should always be a pleasant experience for anyone who appreciates 'em (and collections of such items usually *should* merit a modicum of respect), there's already been a plethora of books devoted to guitars and basses that are considered super-collectible within the vintage guitar phenomenon.

But what about the budget instruments that an untold number of young players cut their musical teeth on when they were teens in the '50s, '60s, and '70s? Jeff Carlisi's right on the money concerning the first time Ed Sullivan presented the Beatles to an American television audience. It was an epiphany (hormonal and otherwise) for an untold number of (primarily male) teenage viewers, many of whom purchased a Sears amp-in-the-case model at their next opportunity.

Moreover, the history of American-made electric guitars includes more than just the instruments made and marketed by "the Big Two" (Gibson and Fender), and even those giants had their share of problems during specific eras. Some U.S. guitar makers were much more prolific than Fender and Gibson combined during the fabled "guitar boom" of the '60s, while other companies, even if they offered (like Ford) "a better idea," ended up as mere flashes-in-the-pan in the musical instrument marketplace.

You'll see plenty of classic and/or rare Fenders and Gibsons in this tome, but you'll also see plenty of clean Harmonys, Kays, and Danelectros, and *there's the rub*: Finding a relatively pristine example of an American-made *budget* guitar is probably a rarer occasion than some folks might think. Many aspiring players may have

bought American-made beginners' instruments in their youth, but upon discovering that they weren't going to be the next George Harrison, Nokie Edwards, or Chet Atkins, may have relegated such instruments to storage, or worse yet, abject neglect. One would expect a frontline Gibson electric guitar from 1961 to have been treated with respect over the decades, but what about a Sears Silvertone model 1421L (made by Harmony, priced at $54.95) of the same vintage?

In addition, there are lots of brands and manufacturers noted herein that may not have gotten an appropriate amount of attention (if any) in the pantheon of American electric guitar history, and perhaps that's particularly important these days. For quite a few years, *approximately 90 percent of the new guitars and basses sold in the United States have been imported instruments* (insert nostalgic and/or jingoistic rumination here).

The other "egalitarian" facet of this book's creation concerned the dozens of persons who got instruments to us for photography. Not only did we get guitars from notable dealers and collectors, we also photographed instruments that belonged to average folks (even some retirees) who happened to own something that fit the format of this presentation. Everything from a rare, custom instrument to a hugely-popular guitar like a Danelectro/Silvertone was photographed in the same location, under the same conditions.

We really appreciate the cooperation of everyone involved with this project, and we hope that the instruments pictured herein will remind readers of a bygone time of gargantuan American guitar production and sales. Hopefully, some of the more-recent examples will demonstrate that U.S. guitar craftsmanship is still viable, even if it's in a distinct minority regarding numbers of instruments.

Enjoy!

Vega Supertron, mid-1940s. $600

Perhaps the definitive example is that of a pawn shop manager who was so naive about electric guitars, she thought archtop electric guitars weren't being made any more, and that all current electric guitars were solidbody instruments.

It might have come as a surprise to her (and to other persons with a minimal interest in electric guitars, business or otherwise) to discover that not only are archtop electrics still being made, attempts to improve the volume of guitars by use of electronic accessories date back to the '20s. Some of the earliest efforts were simply acoustic guitars with microphones stuck in them, and once the guitar pickup began to be developed and refined, the first electric guitar models were more or less based on acoustic models, with a pickup and control knobs stuck on them.

And considering how the evolution of solidbody electric guitars has been indelibly paralleled to the evolution of Rock and Roll (infancy, adolescence, and, uh, "maturity"), it's intriguing to harken back to the previous generation and note that one of the primary reasons electric guitars came into being was an attempt to get a guitarist in a Big Band format to be heard in the mix with other instruments. Look at any number of old black-and-white performances of Big Bands, as seen on nostalgia-oriented cable channels: more times than not, the guitarist will be seen flailing away on a large archtop guitar, desperately trying to compete with the reeds and brass.

So most electric guitars in the first half of the 20th century were electrified cousins of manufacturers' acoustic instruments, and two '40s examples shown here are important from a historical perspective. Boston's Vega company and the original family-owned, New York-based Epiphone organization are no longer in existence—both brands went through ownership changes.

Vega was purchased by Martin in 1970, which sold the brand to a foreign company in 1980. Gibson purchased Epiphone in 1957, and in 1970, shifted the production of standard Epiphone models to the Far East. Of note on these two instruments are the thumbwheel on the left side of the Vega's body (which adjusts the height of the pickup), and the metal logo on the Epiphone's headstock (it can also be found on some earlier Gibson-made Epiphones). However, the bottom line from a manufacturing point of view is that both of these once-viable American brands are not made in the U.S. anymore.

Epiphone Century, mid-1940s.
$600

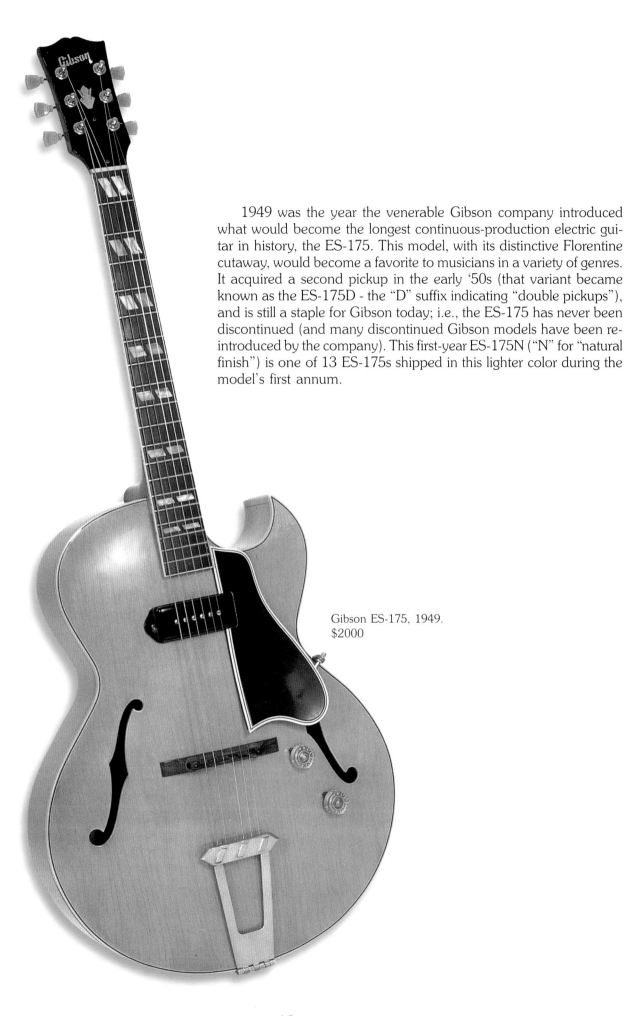

1949 was the year the venerable Gibson company introduced what would become the longest continuous-production electric guitar in history, the ES-175. This model, with its distinctive Florentine cutaway, would become a favorite to musicians in a variety of genres. It acquired a second pickup in the early '50s (that variant became known as the ES-175D - the "D" suffix indicating "double pickups"), and is still a staple for Gibson today; i.e., the ES-175 has never been discontinued (and many discontinued Gibson models have been reintroduced by the company). This first-year ES-175N ("N" for "natural finish") is one of 13 ES-175s shipped in this lighter color during the model's first annum.

Gibson ES-175, 1949.
$2000

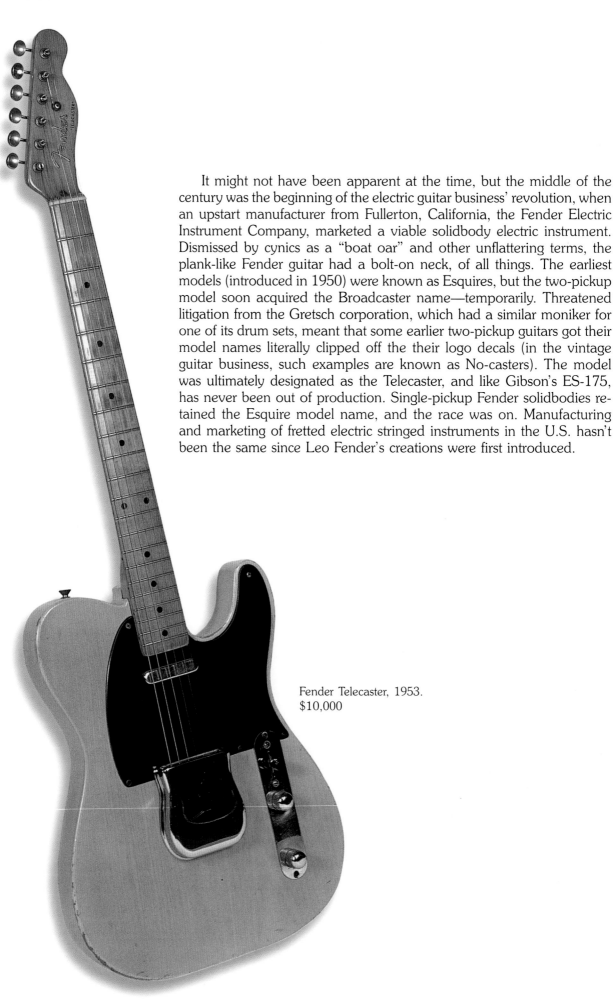

It might not have been apparent at the time, but the middle of the century was the beginning of the electric guitar business' revolution, when an upstart manufacturer from Fullerton, California, the Fender Electric Instrument Company, marketed a viable solidbody electric instrument. Dismissed by cynics as a "boat oar" and other unflattering terms, the plank-like Fender guitar had a bolt-on neck, of all things. The earliest models (introduced in 1950) were known as Esquires, but the two-pickup model soon acquired the Broadcaster name—temporarily. Threatened litigation from the Gretsch corporation, which had a similar moniker for one of its drum sets, meant that some earlier two-pickup guitars got their model names literally clipped off the their logo decals (in the vintage guitar business, such examples are known as No-casters). The model was ultimately designated as the Telecaster, and like Gibson's ES-175, has never been out of production. Single-pickup Fender solidbodies retained the Esquire model name, and the race was on. Manufacturing and marketing of fretted electric stringed instruments in the U.S. hasn't been the same since Leo Fender's creations were first introduced.

Fender Telecaster, 1953.
$10,000

Fender Esquire, 1952. $6500

Fender Precision Bass, 1952. $4500

As if the new Fender electric solidbody guitars didn't shake up the musical instrument marketplace enough, the innovative company turned around and quickly developed a new and unique type of instrument. Leo Fender and his associate, George Fullerton, designed a bass that was played (and shaped) like a solidbody guitar—it even had frets! The revolutionary Precision Bass shoved the large and cumbersome upright "doghouse" bass into immediate obsolescence for many bands. The original P-Bass looked pretty much like a larger version of the Telecaster to most observers (but had double cutaways), and although it's been through more than one transmogrification, it too has never been discontinued by Fender.

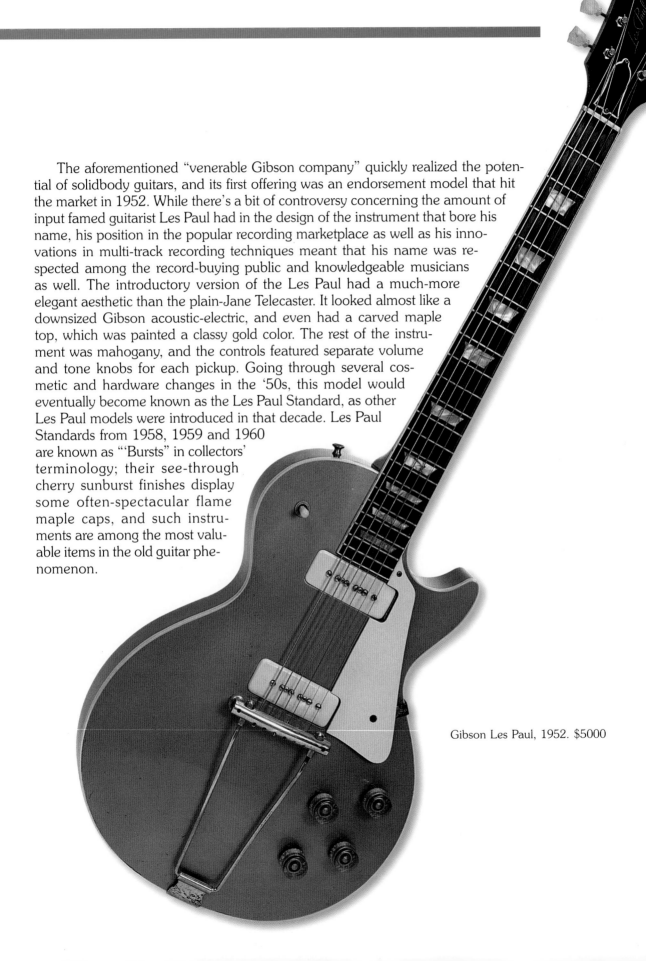

The aforementioned "venerable Gibson company" quickly realized the potential of solidbody guitars, and its first offering was an endorsement model that hit the market in 1952. While there's a bit of controversy concerning the amount of input famed guitarist Les Paul had in the design of the instrument that bore his name, his position in the popular recording marketplace as well as his innovations in multi-track recording techniques meant that his name was respected among the record-buying public and knowledgeable musicians as well. The introductory version of the Les Paul had a much-more elegant aesthetic than the plain-Jane Telecaster. It looked almost like a downsized Gibson acoustic-electric, and even had a carved maple top, which was painted a classy gold color. The rest of the instrument was mahogany, and the controls featured separate volume and tone knobs for each pickup. Going through several cosmetic and hardware changes in the '50s, this model would eventually become known as the Les Paul Standard, as other Les Paul models were introduced in that decade. Les Paul Standards from 1958, 1959 and 1960 are known as "'Bursts" in collectors' terminology; their see-through cherry sunburst finishes display some often-spectacular flame maple caps, and such instruments are among the most valuable items in the old guitar phenomenon.

Gibson Les Paul, 1952. $5000

Fender soon developed another classic model that would become the world's most popular electric guitar in the latter half of the century. Leo Fender, George Fullerton, and Hawaiian musician Freddie Tavares, assisted by the input of Western guitarist Bill Carson (who field-tested a prototype and ultimately worked for the Fender company longer than anyone else, including Leo Fender himself), created the Fender Stratocaster, a contoured and comfortable slick-looking three-pickup guitar that was capable of all sorts of sounds. It's curious that the Strat has gained so much acceptance among rock musicians over the decades, since its innovative vibrato system, utilized with a volume control, was actually supposed to emulate a steel guitar sound, according to Carson. Once again, the Stratocaster has been modified over the years (and at present comes in dozens of styles) but has never been out of the guitar marketplace since it was announced as "Another First for Fender" in a 1954 music magazine ad.

Fender Stratocaster, 1957.
$8000

Harmony H44 Stratotone, 1953.
$300

Vintage snobs may speculate about the presence of this small Harmony Stratotone alongside all of these icons from the seminal days of the American electric guitar phenomenon, but this particular instrument simply exemplifies the fairly-immediate participation of even *budget* guitar manufacturers in the solidbody guitar market. Obviously, the H44 (the first solidbody introduced by Harmony) owes its inspiration to the Gibson Les Paul, right down to its metallic color. It's a one-pickup instrument, but has a small tone bypass switch to allow two distinct sounds at the flip of a switch. The H44 Stratotone was introduced in 1953, and this particular one may be an early example, as its potentiometers date from 1952.

So the advent of the second half of the 1900s heralded a new and exciting era of guitar music. The development of the solidbody electric guitar, coupled with the emergence of Rock and Roll, provided vast opportunities for American guitar manufacturers, and "the Big Two" began their battle for the top of the pyramid. Other companies scrambled to get their share of the action, and other *new* builders also entered the fray. It was an exciting time, but before it was over, many guitar companies (some of which had been in business for decades) would close their doors permanently.

17

STANDARDS

Right or wrong, the second half of the 20th century was pretty much a two-company battle for dominance in the American electric guitar market. That's still the case, in spite of more than one change in ownership for Fender and Gibson, and in spite of the previously-noted avalanche of imported instruments (both Fender and Gibson import a large quantity of guitars and basses themselves, for that matter). Nevertheless, a standard procedure (pun intended) whenever classic American guitars and basses are being discussed is to cite the efforts of "the Big Two" throughout the decades, including their innovations over the years that refined the sound and reliability of electric fretted instruments.

FENDER

A half-century after its intriguing introduction, a basic Fender Telecaster still had a slab-like body, master volume and tone knobs, and a pickup toggle switch. It's had numerous improvements to its hardware and electronics, of course, but it also still has a raucous, twangy sound that's just about inimitable (Esquires were gone by early '70). In the mid-'50s, the color of those models changed from a butterscotch finish to a lighter blond color, and white pickguards replaced black ones. In 1959, the entire Fender guitar line began to get rosewood fingerboards laminated to their maple necks. The position markers on the original rosewood fretboards were made from a matte-finished material, and are known as "clay dots" in vintage jargon. Here are a 1961 Telecaster and a 1963 Esquire with all of the subsequent construction and cosmetic changes the original Fender company instituted to their groundbreaking solidbody models. The cigarette burn on the Esquire's headstock is a definitive time-warp "badge"...

Telecaster, 1961. $5000

Esquire, 1963. $3000

The purchase of Fender by CBS in 1965 heralded a lot of changes to the California company and its products, and while finishes came and went on all guitars and basses (and maple fretboards became available again), the Telecaster was relatively unaffected in its construction, compared to some other frontline models. A natural finish, ash-bodied Telecaster from 1978 looks, plays, and sounds a lot like its older relatives; however, one source reports that this instrument is somewhat unique, in that rosewood fingerboards were only found on an estimated 20% of Fender's standard production Telecasters when this guitar was built.

Telecaster, 1978. $900

The first variant of the Telecaster was introduced in 1959, in tandem with the change to rosewood fretboards. Custom Telecasters had an alder body, a sunburst finish, and front-and-back binding. Electronically they were the same as their standard Tele siblings.

CBS's acquisition of Fender ultimately resulted in the development and marketing of other versions of the Telecaster, and the first new model came along in 1968. The new Telecaster Thinline wasn't a skinnier instrument; instead, it had a hollowed-out body (made of ash or mahogany) that resulted in a guitar that weighed about half of what a solidbody Tele weighed. Cosmetically, it also featured a single f-hole and a different pickguard silhouette, but once again, this guitar was an electronic clone of other Telecasters.

Custom Telecaster, 1960. $7000

Telecaster Thinline, 1969. $2500

Stratocasters fared quite differently concerning their cosmetics and construction over the years. Prior to the 1959 rosewood fingerboard production change, a Strat's two-tone sunburst finish had been altered to include a reddish third color between its yellow and dark brown colors. Some early attempts at creating the three-tone finish stumbled—the red pigment faded, causing the finish to revert to a two-tone color! Note the differences in the finish on this 1963 Stratocaster and the 1957 model seen earlier.

Stratocaster, 1963. $5000

Stratocaster, 1966. $5500

Further cosmetic changes on Strats occurred around the time Fender became a CBS subsidiary. The model acquired a larger headstock (which was fine with Bill Carson, who'd always favored such a look), and pearloid position markers replaced "clay dots." This 1966 instrument sports a Candy Apple Red Custom Color finish, as well as a gold "transition" logo, but that term is a bit of a misnomer, having nothing to do with the CBS purchase—Fender had actually begun using such a logo on instruments as early as 1960.

Subsequent frontline guitar models introduced by Fender in the late '50s and the '60s were ultimately less successful for the rapidly-growing California manufacturer. Some instruments had commendable innovations, but most didn't have a stereotypical "sound" associated with them, as was the case with Telecasters and Stratocasters.

Fender's next major introduction in the electric guitar market (aside from some student models that the company began to ship in 1956) was the Jazzmaster, which was proffered in 1958. Decidedly different from Telecasters and Stratocasters, this new instrument offered several new and logical refinements for a solidbody electric guitar. Its body was an offset style, which was comfortable if a musician was sitting down. Jazzmasters also had a different type of vibrato system, but the Stratocaster's vibrato would emerge as the more dependable and successful mechanism. Yet another intriguing innovation was circuitry that included two independent sets of volume and tone controls, allowing for instant changes from one sound to another by flipping a switch. The Jazzmaster garnered its share of notable endorsers, but hardly any of them were in the burgeoning Rock and Roll phenomenon until instrumental guitar music by groups like the Ventures and California surf music bands called attention to the entire Fender guitar line in a big way. The Jazzmaster shown here is in the model's first configuration, with controls mounted in an anodized aluminum pickguard.

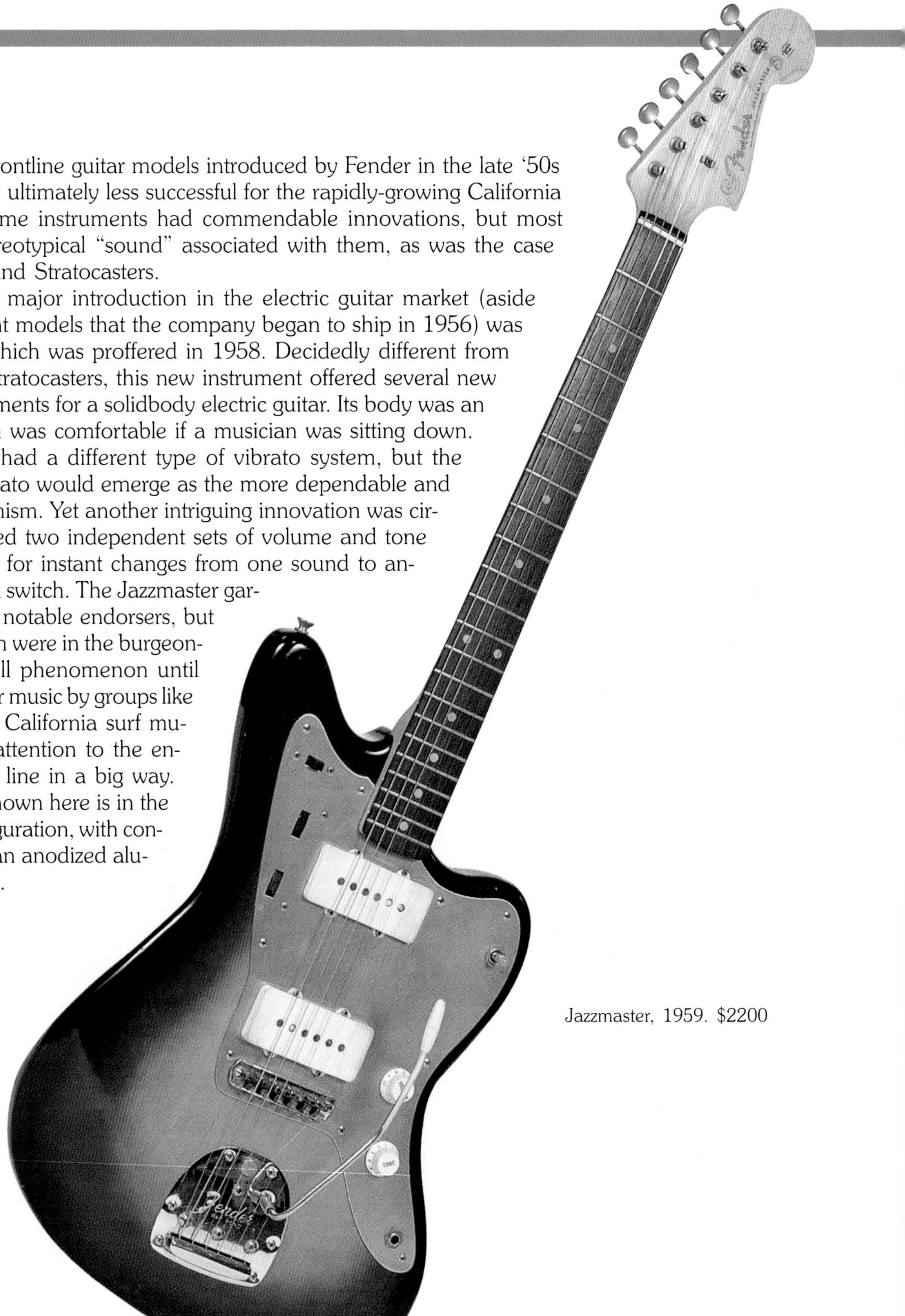

Jazzmaster, 1959. $2200

The Jazzmaster's slightly-shorter sibling was the Jaguar, the only mainline guitar introduced with a 24-inch scale instead of the usual 25½-inch scale found on other professional-grade Fenders. Jaguars hit the musical instrument marketplace in 1962, and, like Jazzmasters, offered pre-set volume and tone compatibility, but important differences besides scale length included more switches (i.e., more complexity?), and a flip-up mute. Its pickups were surrounded by notched metal parts that looked somewhat like a bear trap. The first-year-example shown here is finished in Fiesta Red, one of Fender's most enduring Custom Colors (note the matching headstock). The later version has block-shaped fretboard markers.

Jaguar, 1962. $2500

Jaguar, 1966. $1100

What appears to be a baby guitar is actually an Electric Mandolin, introduced by Fender in 1956. These tiny instruments were never popular, and unlike standard mandolins, which had eight strings, Electric Mandolins only had four strings. These diminutive solidbodies were unusual, and their rarity makes them interesting to some collectors, particularly persons who are also fans of Western Swing and Country music.

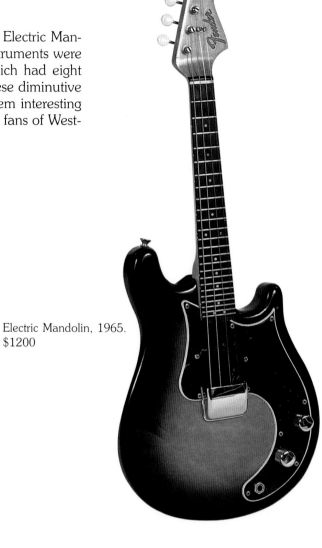

Electric Mandolin, 1965.
$1200

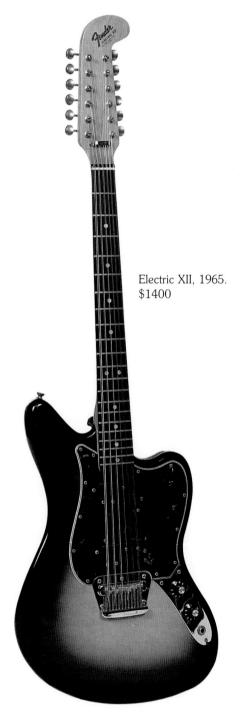

Electric XII, 1965.
$1400

During the '60s, the Fender company developed and marketed other unique electric guitars and basses, and the Electric XII was introduced in 1965, soon after the acquisition of Fender by CBS (it had already been in the R&D pipeline prior to the CBS purchase), and was apparently an attempt to capitalize on the folk music phenomenon. Its pickups were a split, oval-shaped type, and the headstock silhouette of the Electric XII is sometimes referred to as a "hockey stick" shape. Unfortunately, this model seemed to come onto the market too late, as the folk music fad was already in decline by the mid-'60s. However, the Electric XII is quite easy to play, compared to some of its twelve-string competitors. It has been reported that Led Zeppelin guitarist Jimmy Page used this model on the introduction to "Stairway to Heaven," one of the most popular songs in rock music history, which means, of course, the Electric XII may have been *heard* more often than some of its twelve-string competitors.

The first major series of instruments introduced during the "CBS era" for Fender that did not have the involvement of Leo Fender himself was the Coronado collection of guitars and basses. These hollowbody electrics were supposed to compete with Gibson's ES-335-type instruments, but fared badly. One plausible reason was that Fender had built its reputation as a solidbody electric guitar company, and Coronados may have seemed out-of-place to many players. Coronados had bolt-on necks like other Fenders, but once again, lacked a distinctive sound to attract serious guitarists. The series was such a dud that subsequent series, called Wildwoods and Antiguas, had to be offered in different finishes, etc., just to use up parts. The failure of this first aggregation of instruments that were not affiliated with Leo Fender was a harbinger of problems that would plague CBS/Fender for almost two decades.

Coronado XII, 1967.
$600

Precision, 1955.
$3000

Then there were Fender's further offerings in the solidbody electric bass facet of the stringed instrument market. The folks in Fullerton had introduced the radically different Precision Bass to acclaim and success in the middle of the century, and their follow-up innovations in the still-in-its-infancy electric bass market were most likely monitored very closely, by musicians and competitors alike.

In the mid-'50s, the P-Bass received contouring to its body, a la the Stratocaster. Around the same time, the model's cosmetics changed from a butterscotch finish and black pickguard to a sunburst finish and white pickguard as standard appointments, but the example shown here is in the optional blond finish (the same color that Telecasters acquired as a standard finish back then).

In 1957, the Precision Bass acquired the basic silhouette that is still the standard today. Like its six-string associates, the P-Bass has undergone improvement to its electronics, hardware, and construction techniques, but it still looks pretty much the same as it did the year Sputnik was launched by the USSR.

This 1966 sunburst finish Precision is perhaps *the* definitive electric bass in *the* definitive color scheme for the chronology of the instrument itself, not just for the brand and model. Over the decades, there's no telling how many bassists in any number of popular music genres utilized a three-tone sunburst P-Bass with a tortoise-shell pickguard. Notable examples include James Jamerson, who laid down the foundation for numerous Motown hits, Tim Bogert (Vanilla Fudge, Cactus), Donald "Duck" Dunn (Booker T & the MGs), and the most recorded electric bassist in history, Carol Kaye. Even Elvis Presley was seen brandishing a sunburst Precision (if not actually playing it) in a publicity photo for one of his movies. Fender basses were also available in Custom Colors, and here's a gold P-Bass that's also a '66 model.

Precision, 1966.
$1600

Precision, 1966.
$3200

26

This 1973 Precision Bass notes the return of a maple fingerboard (as an option), and it was around the time that this bass was made that Fender began to manufacture some of their mainline instruments with a radically different neck attachment and truss rod system, but the Precision wasn't one of 'em; standard P-Basses have maintained a four-bolt neck attachment system for throughout their history (see "Sordid Seventies Samples & Early Eighties Oddities" for details). The ash grain on this natural-finished Precision is quite attractive.

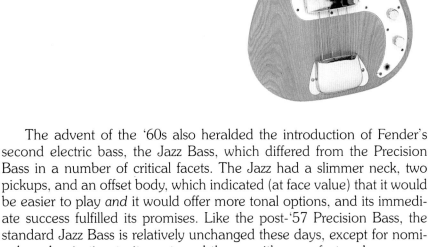

Precision, 1973.
$850

Jazz, 1966.
$2100

The advent of the '60s also heralded the introduction of Fender's second electric bass, the Jazz Bass, which differed from the Precision Bass in a number of critical facets. The Jazz had a slimmer neck, two pickups, and an offset body, which indicated (at face value) that it would be easier to play *and* it would offer more tonal options, and its immediate success fulfilled its promises. Like the post-'57 Precision Bass, the standard Jazz Bass is relatively unchanged these days, except for nominal modernization to its parts and the way it's manufactured.

But both of the Jazz Basses shown here *do* have some short-lived cosmetic incongruities that would be of interest to vintage guitar enthusiasts. The 1966 variant is an example of the Jazz Bass that had neck binding with dot markers on its fretboard; such a combination only lasted for about a year until block position markers replaced dots. Again, it's got that classic combination of a three-tone sunburst with a tortoiseshell pickguard, and its chrome handrest (covering the bass pickup) and its large bridge cover—a.k.a. "ashtray" (covering the bridge and bridge pickup)—have been removed, exposing the pickups.

27

This 1973 Jazz Bass, on the other hand, has some visuals that go in the opposite direction from its 1966 counterpart. It's finished in a milky-but-attractive see-through blond color (notice how the tortoise-shell pickguard on this one really seems to conflict with the color of the body, as opposed to "coordinating," for lack of a better term, with a three-tone sunburst finish). Its maple fretboard has black block markers, and the neck is bound in black as well. This ugly idea (which, admittedly, would make for easy reference when the instrument was being played) wasn't around for long. The handrest and bridge cover are installed on this Jazz, and the latter piece of hardware validates why it received the "ashtray" nickname.

Jazz, 1973.
$1300

Les Paul Custom, 1955.
$5000

GIBSON

Unlike Fender, which opted to develop and introduce different (and theoretically, "improved") guitar models during the '50s, Gibson's primary strategy with their solidbody efforts during that decade was to market different Les Paul variants. The first new model was the Custom, a step-up instrument offered in an elegant black finish on an all mahogany body (no maple cap, as found on the original Les Paul model). Other upgrade features included an ebony fretboard with block-shaped position markers, gold hardware, binding on the top and back edges of the body, and a "split-diamond" inlay on the head-stock. The Custom was also the first Les Paul to receive a tune-a-matic bridge and stop tailpiece, but one of its most unusual features was the installation of two different pickups – the bridge pickup was a P-90, as found on the original Les Paul, but the neck pickup was an Alnico V model with rectangular-shaped polepieces.

The Les Paul Custom was introduced in late 1953, and in mid-1954, Gibson went the opposite direction concerning features (and price) when the Les Paul Junior was marketed. It still retained the series' single-cutaway silhouette, but its body was plank-like (no carved top) with a sunburst finish. A single P-90 was screwed onto its top, and its position markers were simple dots.

Les Paul Jr., 1957.
$1600

Les Paul Special, 1957.
$3700

A lighter-colored Junior was marketed separately as the Les Paul TV, and 1955 saw the introduction of what was essentially a two-pickup Junior known as the Les Paul Special. It, too, came in the light finish, known as "limed mahogany."

The Les Paul Custom, Junior, and the '57 Special are shown in the original configurations of those respective models. These two '59 Specials exemplify the cosmetic and/or construction changes that all Les Paul models went through during the '50s. Note the by-then-standard cherry finish on a double-cutaway body (the Junior had affected the same finish and silhouette as well). This ¾-size Special is *hyper*-rare; one source reports that only twelve were made in 1959.

Les Paul Special ¾, 1959. $2000

Les Paul Special, 1959. $3000

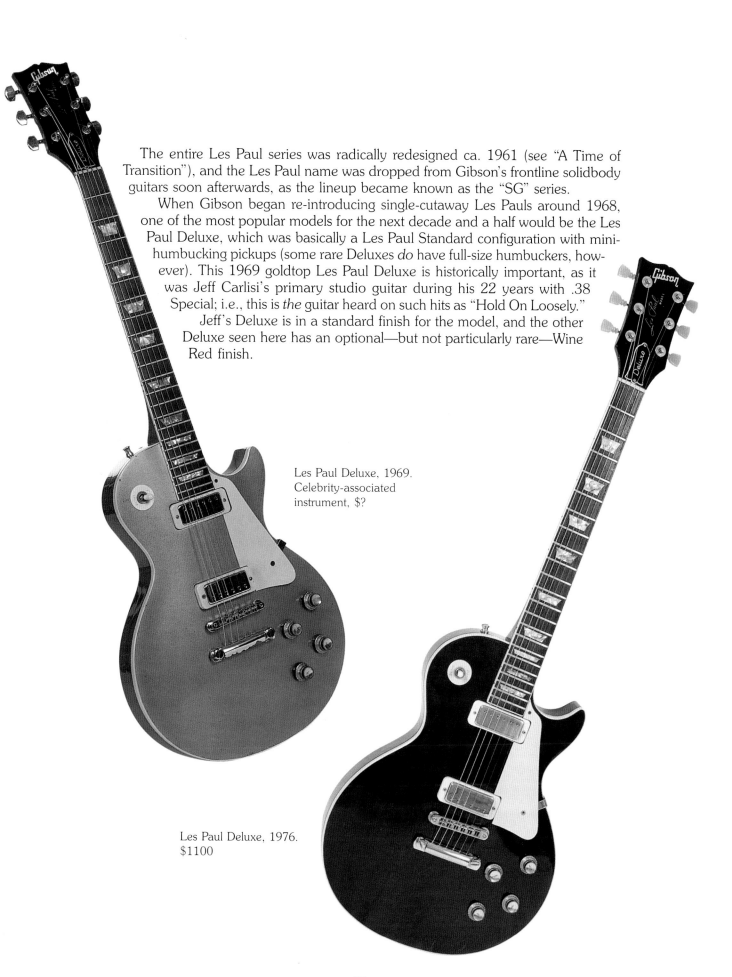

The entire Les Paul series was radically redesigned ca. 1961 (*see* "A Time of Transition"), and the Les Paul name was dropped from Gibson's frontline solidbody guitars soon afterwards, as the lineup became known as the "SG" series.

When Gibson began re-introducing single-cutaway Les Pauls around 1968, one of the most popular models for the next decade and a half would be the Les Paul Deluxe, which was basically a Les Paul Standard configuration with mini-humbucking pickups (some rare Deluxes *do* have full-size humbuckers, however). This 1969 goldtop Les Paul Deluxe is historically important, as it was Jeff Carlisi's primary studio guitar during his 22 years with .38 Special; *i.e.*, this is *the* guitar heard on such hits as "Hold On Loosely."

Jeff's Deluxe is in a standard finish for the model, and the other Deluxe seen here has an optional—but not particularly rare—Wine Red finish.

Les Paul Deluxe, 1969.
Celebrity-associated
instrument, $?

Les Paul Deluxe, 1976.
$1100

The rekindled interest in Les Paul models motivated Gibson to introduce all sorts of variants in the '70s, and such is still the case for the company's flagship series. They've been made (and/or *are* being made) in limited editions, signature models, historical re-issues (some of which are pretty accurate reproductions; however, the "re-issue" term has been applied somewhat loosely to certain models that have been marketed as such), "Smartwood" models (exotic non-endangered wood construction), "Lite" models (thinner body), and even tie-dyed models!

As for unique models from the '70s, the Artisan was, as is obvious, one of the most cosmetically-fancy production Les Pauls ever made. The inlay on its fretboard and headstock resembles what would usually be seen on some Gibson banjos. It also had gold hardware, and this example has an optional third pickup. Interestingly, the Artisan was reported to have been introduced in 1976, but this one has a serial number that belongs to a system that was discontinued in 1975. Artisans themselves were discontinued in 1982.

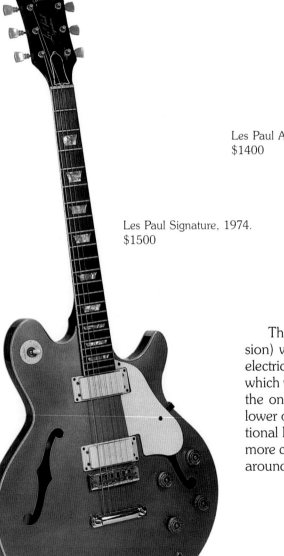

Les Paul Artisan, mid-1970s.
$1400

Les Paul Signature, 1974.
$1500

The Les Paul Signature (which had a companion bass version) was the only Les Paul that was produced in a thinline electric-acoustic archtop style. Note the asymmetrical cutaways, which were unique to the model (the upper cutaway resembles the one found on such instruments as the ES-335, while the lower one resembles the treble cutaway horn found on a traditional Les Paul solidbody). The Signature's controls were a bit more complex, and it even had two jacks. The model was only around for about five years ('73 to '78).

Even this '77 Les Paul Special is unique, in that it's a "pre-catalog" guitar—this version reportedly went into production in 1978. It's got a tune-a-matic bridge and stop tailpiece, which original Specials didn't have (see the '59 models), and this particular example has a dot fret marker on the first fret.

Les Paul Special, 1977.
$750

ES-175, 1952.
$2000

Gibson didn't have an exclusive patent on the pointed Florentine cutaway seen on many of its acoustic and electric guitars, but some of the instruments with that silhouette turned out to be important models in the company's history. The Kalamazoo factory had already introduced an electric guitar with a cutaway before the ES-175 was announced in 1949, but as noted earlier, that model has been in continuous production for over half a century.

And here are several ES-175s from several decades. This 1952 example is basically the same as the 1949 example seen in the "Progenitors" chapter, except for its more-often-seen standard sunburst finish.

This 1964 ES-175D is in a somewhat lighter sunburst finish (sometimes referred to as an "ice tea" sunburst). It has humbucking pickups (which the model acquired in 1957) as well as an artsy-looking tailpiece.

ES-175D, 1964.
$3500

Then there's this early '70s ES-175DN. "Early '70s" is about as close as we can get to dating this example, since Gibson's serial number system from 1970 to 1975 didn't make much sense (this system was the one to which the serial number on the Les Paul Artisan cited earlier belonged). This guitar is in mint condition, and the name of the person who was probably the original owner has been routed into the pickguard. Its laminated maple body doesn't show off any figuring in the wood, but the grain itself is quite distinguishable. Adding to the intrigue of the name on the pickguard was the discovery of a number of items in the guitar case when this writer encountered this instrument in a Georgia pawn shop. The contents included a capo, two receipts showing the down payment and payoff amounts on the instrument when it was purchased in San Diego in 1975 (was it new or used then?), around 20 receipts from what was apparently a mail-order guitar course, a handwritten song list, and *a Wes Montgomery Jazz Chord Method* book. Finding such "goodies" in a guitar case is sort of a "bonus" when enthusiasts are sussing out old guitars, and when a nice instrument such as this one comes out for retail at a pawn shop because it wasn't redeemed, it's only natural to wonder what kind of sad story—legitimate or not—caused it to end up for sale in such a business establishment.

Sharp-eyed observers will note that the other natural-finish electric guitar with a Florentine cutaway isn't another instrument like the one described in the previous paragraph; it's skinnier, and is accordingly known as an ES-175TDN ("T" = "thinline"). That's the only difference between it and its full-depth big brothers, but the thinline version of the ES-175 was only made from 1976 to 1979 (this example is a first-year model).

What appears at first glance to be a "downsized" version of the ES-175 (as opposed to "skinnier," in the case of the ES-175TDN) is actually a different model, the ES-140 ¾. It's probably logical that it resembles the original ES-175, since this diminutive electric guitar was introduced in 1950. It lacked the ES-175's double parallelogram-shaped fret markers, though; they probably would have looked aesthetically awkward on this smaller instrument, so simple dot markers are on the fretboard instead. Its scale was 22 ¾ inches (two inches shorter than most other Gibson instruments' scales), and it underwent an interesting transmogrification in the late '50s. The full-depth version of this instrument was discontinued, and was supplanted by a thinline version (ES-140 3/4T); i.e., a choice of body depths was not offered.

ES-175DN, early '70s.
$1900

ES-175TDN, 1976.
$1500

ES-140 ¾, ca. 1952.
$1100

The short-lived ES-225T (1955-1958) wasn't particularly distinguished as an electric instrument, but it's quite important from a historical perspective, as it was the first Gibson model designed and marketed as a thinline electric guitar. There wasn't a full-depth version of this model that preceded it (although, as noted with the ES-175TDN, such a scenario did happen with other Gibson models). Note the not-so-dependable combination long trapeze tailpiece/bridge unit, as found on the original Les Paul solidbody guitar. The model was offered in a two-pickup version that was introduced in 1956, and about the only person of distinction seen playing one was Niki Sullivan, the other guitar player in Buddy Holly & the Crickets; he's seen with his sunburst ES-225TD on the cover of *The Chirping Crickets* album. So while not it's not highly-sought by collectors, the ES-225T was the first instrument of its type introduced by Gibson.

ES-225T, 1955.
$800

ES-335TN, 1959. Celebrity-associated guitar, $?

1958 must have been an intriguing year for Gibson. Probably stereotyped by many musicians as "Kalamazoo curmudgeons" (or words to that effect), the veteran guitar manufacturer struck back on more than one "front" during the year the Space Race officially began (the U.S. launched Explorer I on January 31st). One effort, that of making and marketing "modernistic"-looking solidbody electric guitars, fizzled out quite quickly, but Gibson's introduction of a "semi-hollow"/"semi-solid" electric guitar was an important innovation in the chronology of electric guitar manufacturing. The instruments that resulted from Gibson's research and development are the models of which then-president Ted McCarty is the proudest (McCarty presided over Gibson from 1948 to 1965, during what will most likely be considered the company's "glory days" regarding its contributions to guitar construction and marketing).

ES-335TDC, 1963.

ES-335TD, 1967.

Gibson had introduced thinline electrics a few years earlier, and now sought to bridge the gap between hollowbody electric guitars and solidbodies with a new design. The new series had not only an unique double-rounded cutaway silhouette on a thinline body; the interior of the body contained a maple block designed to give such a guitar a brighter sound while lessening the possibility of feedback (a la a solidbody), while maintaining a bit of acoustic resonance (thanks to the f-holes) and the lesser weight of hollowbody electrics. It proved to be a happy marriage of styles.

The ES-335 was and is the most popular Gibson semi-solid (it's still in production), and the three examples shown here exemplify some of its important refinements over the years. Jeff Carlisi's 1959 natural-finish guitar, seen on the previous page, is a classic, and was known as the ES-335TN when it was made. Even though ES-335s had two pickups from the get-go, it appears that the "D" suffix wasn't applied to them until 1960. The original configuration of the '59 model includes a stop tailpiece, dot fretboard markers, and a long pickguard that extends slightly past the bridge. The 1963 ES-335TDC has block fret markers, a shorter pickguard, and an original factory-installed Bigsby vibrato. A so-called "Custom Made" plaque actually covers the stud holes where a stop tailpiece would normally be found. Another suffix incongruity with Gibson's semi-solid series is "C"—on these instruments, it signifies "cherry finish," not "cutaway." By 1967, the model had acquired a trapeze tailpiece, as seen on this sunburst instrument. Most of the ES-335 variants made by Gibson these days have stop tailpieces.

37

Like Fender, Gibson apparently reacted to the popularity of the folk-rock genre by introducing a 12-string version of the ES-335, but the model was only in production from 1965 to 1971. The ES-335-12 was pretty much a basic ES-335 with appropriate alternative parts to accommodate the additional strings (as noted earlier, Fender developed an entire new instrument). Gibson's initial contribution to the electric 12-string market was seen in the hands of more players than Fender's Electric XII, and British guitarist Steve Howe of Yes and Asia fame played one on Asia's "Only Time Will Tell."

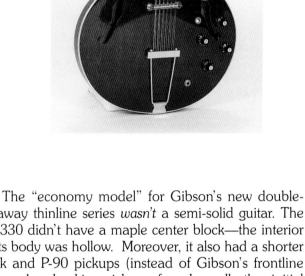

ES-335-12, 1968. $1300

ES-330TD, 1961. $2500

ES-330TDC, 1964. $1700

The "economy model" for Gibson's new double-cutaway thinline series *wasn't* a semi-solid guitar. The ES-330 didn't have a maple center block—the interior of its body was hollow. Moreover, it also had a shorter neck and P-90 pickups (instead of Gibson's frontline humbucking pickups, found on all other initial semi-solid guitar models). The ES-330 was also available in a one-pickup model for a brief time. The examples shown here point out a couple of cosmetic evolutions for the model— note the black P-90s on the '61 ES-330, and the chrome P-90s on the '64, as well as the different fretmarkers. Interestingly, both models also have factory vibratos, which is highly unusual for this model. In particular, the '61 variant is quite unique, in that it has a short-lived vibrato system that was usually found on early '60s "transitional" Les Pauls (see "A Time of Transition").

The ES-125 was Gibson's "workhorse" archtop electric for quite a few years, and was made in quite a few configurations. The model had originally been introduced as the ES-100 in the '30s, was renamed the ES-125 in the early '40s, and went out of production during World War II. It was reintroduced in 1946 and went through all kinds of variants during its tenure of nearly a quarter-century. A basic ES-125 was a full-depth model with a single P-90 pickup, but it was ultimately available with a cutaway (add a "C" suffix to the model number), two pickups (add a "D" suffix), and a thinline version (add a "T" suffix). Moreover, other ES-125 models had combinations of the features the aforementioned suffixes describe *in all possible variants* (except for one smaller-bodied ES-125).

All of the 125s seen here are thinline variants, and here's the earliest and simplest model, a non-cutaway, single-pickup ES-125T, which was introduced in the mid-'50s.

The Florentine cutaway on this 1961 ES-125TC might make for some confusion regarding its resemblance to an ES-225T. However, in addition to the differences in the pickup location as well as the more-traditional separate bridge and tailpiece, ES-125s had an unbound fretboard and a gold silkscreen logo, whereas the ES-225T had a bound fingerboard and a pearl logo. Curiously, *thinline* cutaway variants of this series were introduced in 1960, whereas *full-depth* cutaway models (ES-125C and ES-125CD)didn't come along until 1966. This ES-125TC has a first-year-of-availability cherry sunburst finish.

The two-pickup ES-125TDC is a favorite of blues guitarist George Thorogood ("Bad to the Bone," "Move It On Over," and other hits), who claims it's the only guitar he can play because of his aggressive playing style. Thorogood notes that the strings on his ES-125TDCs are fairly high off of the body of the instrument, which gives his right hand plenty of "clearance," for lack of a better term. The guitarist's arsenal of ES-125TDCs usually totals eight—four frontline guitars in four different tunings, plus a backup for each. "For some reason," noted Thorogood's longtime guitar tech, J.J. Liberatto, "we have the most luck with the ones made before 1966." Almost all of Thorogood's stage instruments have been refinished white. The ES-125TDC shown here is a '64 model with an added tune-a-matic bridge.

ES-125T, ca. 1964. $550

ES-125TC, 1961. $800

ES-125TDC, 1964. $800

In the same "downsized" category as the ES-140 ¾ (which, as noted earlier, assumed a thinline-only style as the ES-140T ¾ circa 1957) was the ES-125T ¾, which had the same body width and scale length as its forebear. It was only made in a single pickup, non-cutaway, thinline style. Cute, ain't it?

ES125T ¾, 1959. $700

Of course, Gibson would design and market high-end, ornate archtop electrics during the halcyon days of American guitar manufacturing, and one of its most unique upgrade instruments was the Byrdland, which was designed with the input of guitarists Billy Byrd and Hank Garland (its name is a combination of their surnames). The model was a thinline-style instrument, debuting soon after the ES-225T; in fact, both instruments were introduced to musical instrument dealers at a July 1955 NAMM (National Association of Music Merchandisers) show. The Byrdland offered an unusually short 23 1/2 inch scale on a thin neck, multiple binding, gold-plated hardware, an ebony fretboard, and a "flowerpot"/ "torch" headstock inlay. Byrdlands have been made with Florentine or Venetian cutaways, and are a favorite of players as diverse as Roy Clark and Ted Nugent.

Byrdland, 1977. $2500

The ES-350T had premiered as the ES-350, a full-depth model with one pickup and a 25½-inch scale in 1947. The ES-350 was Gibson's first electric guitar with a cutaway, and had the "P" suffix added to its model number (for "Premier") when it debuted. It eventually acquired two pickups, and in 1955, a thinline version of the model was introduced as a less-expensive alternative to the Byrdland, and like its fancier thinline cousin, the ES-350T sported a 23½" scale. The full-size ES-350 was discontinued soon after the ES-350T appeared, and like some of the earlier ES-335s and similar semi-solid models, the ES-350T didn't get a "D" suffix in its model number until some time after it was introduced, even though it had two pickups from Day One of its history.

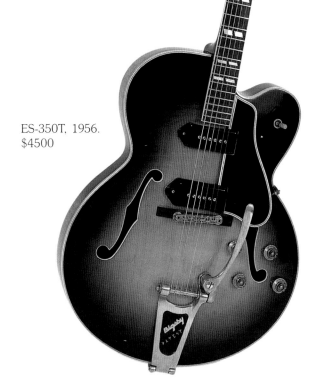

ES-350T, 1956.
$4500

ES-120T, 1964. $550

The nadir of Gibson's archtop electrics was occupied by the ES-120T. As its model number notes, it was only offered in a non-cutaway, single pickup style, yet its electronics were unique (if not necessarily endearing). Its pickup was a single-coil model, as found on Gibson's Melody Maker solidbody guitars of the same era. All of the electronics—pickup, controls, jack, and wiring, were installed in a "plump"-looking pickguard that mounted to the top of the guitar body as a complete unit. Sure, such a concept was efficient and economical, but some cynics might opine that the pickguard looks like it's about to give birth to a litter of guitar picks…

Gibson also made some flat-top electric-acoustic guitars, and its most famous model was the J-160E ("E" = "electric"), due the use of such an instrument by the Beatles. Its pickup was mounted where the fretboard meets the top, and its trapezoid inlay that begins on the first fret is somewhat unique.

J-160E, 1960. $2200

Trini Lopez Standard, 1965.
$1500

Gibson has produced its share of endorsement models over the decades, and in some situations, has "double-dipped"—certain artists have their own version of a Les Paul model, for example. Latin crooner Trini Lopez was more noted for his singing than his guitar prowess, but that didn't deter Gibson from introducing more than one Trini Lopez model in the '60s. This 1965 Trini Lopez Standard was the most popular variant; note the similarity in the body silhouette and electronics to an ES-335. This instrument also has diamond-shaped f-holes, split-diamond-shaped fret markers, and a six-on-a-side headstock that looks quite "Fender-ish". Other (and rarer) Gibson endorsement models from the early-to-mid-'60s included guitars bearing the names of Johnny Smith, Tal Farlow, and Barney Kessel. The Trini Lopez Deluxe looked a lot like the Barney Kessel models, but the Trini Lopez Standard was more popular than any of the rest.

Gibson's mainline solidbody series in the '60s was the venerable SG (for "solid guitar") aggregation. Some instruments with this new sharp-pointed, double-cutaway silhouette actually appeared for a brief name bearing the Les Paul moniker (see "A Time of Transition"), before Paul's endorsement agreement was discontinued.

Throughout their initial decade of production, SGs followed the "Custom-Standard-Special-Junior" lineup designations and features of their Les Paul predecessors (and the lighter-colored Junior was called the SG-TV). The SG Custom still had the fanciest appointments, including three humbucking pickups, which the original Les Paul Custom had acquired in the late '50s. The SG Standard had two humbuckers, the SG Special had two P-90s, and the SG Junior had one P-90, as had been the case for the corresponding Les Paul model each SG replaced. Some standard finishes were different, however—SG Customs were white (as were SG-TVs), Standards were cherry, Specials came in cherry *or* white, and Juniors were cherry. Walnut finishes appeared on some instruments as the decade came to a close.

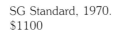

SG Standard, 1970.
$1100

SG Jr., 1965. $900

The original-configuration SG junior shown above has a Gibson Vibrola, which the company introduced around the time the SG series itself premiered. The Vibrola was less complex than a Bigsby vibrato—Gibson's innovation simply relied on a flexible piece of metal, therefore it was *even less dependable* than a Bigsby regarding the instrument remaining in tune.

SGs underwent a minor cosmetic change in 1966. The pickguard on all models was enlarged to extend over both sides of the instrument's face; accordingly, pickups poked up *through* the new, larger pickguards. This 1970 SG Standard has all of the standard features found on the model, including a fancy tailpiece extension (engraved with the Gibson name and a lyre).

However, 1970 may have been the last great year for SGs, as it was the final year of the original configurations. Beginning in '71, Gibson initiated all sorts of changes to the SG lineup, scrambling names, features, etc. It proved to be a debacle, and some new variants didn't last long at all. Many '70s SGs suffered from the same problems that afflicted other Gibson models in that notorious decade (see the chapter titled "Sordid Seventies Samples and Early Eighties Oddities" for details). The only reason this '74 SG Special appears in *this* chapter is because it has the same moniker as a respected forebear. Nevertheless, this '70s model has mini-humbucking pickups in plastic covers, small block markers, and an ugly, dark finish—consider this a sample of what's to come later.

SG Special, 1974.
$800

Flying V, 1974.
$1500

During the '60s and '70s, Gibson occasionally produced instruments which had silhouettes based on their original, late '50s "modernistic" guitars, although the cosmetics, finishes, and even the wood were usually different from the earliest incarnations. Here's a nice, natural-finish mahogany Flying V that dates from 1974.

The most unique series introduced in the '60s by Gibson was the redoubtable Firebird collection. Original Firebirds, which premiered in 1963, are called "reverse" models because they look like flipped-over Fenders. They were the first Gibsons built with neck-through construction, and their headstocks had banjo-type tuners. The VII, V, III, and I models corresponded roughly to the Custom-Standard-Special-Junior designations concerning features, but all models had mini-humbuckers with no polepieces. A matching bass series, Thunderbirds, had a Fenderish 34-inch scale (a first for Gibson). Jeff Carlisi's '63 Firebird VII is extremely rare; its original black finish wasn't even on Gibson's Custom Color charts for Firebirds (a sunburst finish was standard). The absence of a red Firebird logo on the pickguard indicates that this is a very early example of the model.

Firebird VII, 1963.
Celebrity-associated guitar
+ ultra-rare color, $?

Firebird I, 1968.
$1100

So-called "non-reverse" Firebirds came along circa 1965, and *didn't* follow the previously-established Custom-Standard-Special-Junior "guidelines." Firebird VIIs and Vs had mini-humbuckers, but Firebird IIIs and Is had P-90s. The nickname of this second-generation series came about because they had a more "normal" silhouette, regular tuning keys (six-on-a-side), and set-in necks. In other words, they looked more like Fenders. A 12-string Firebird was available in this edition, but the entire lineup was uninspiring. This Firebird I looks somewhat "ordinary" compared to other brands and models, and its slider-type pickup switch was undependable as well. It goes without saying that "reverse" Firebirds are much more desirable in the vintage market than "non-reverse" Firebirds.

45

Gibson also tended to play "catch up" with Fender when it came to the new instrument in the marketplace, the electric bass, just as the Kalamazoo titan had done with the upstart California manufacturer's solidbody electric guitars. The first model offered by Gibson was a violin-shaped instrument that debuted in 1953, but only 546 were shipped by the time it was discontinued in 1958. However, that instrument (and subsequent Gibson basses) differed from Fender's models in a noticeable way: The scale of Gibson's frontline models for the '50s and '60s was 30½ inches (Thunderbirds excepted), a full three-and-a-half inches shorter than Fender's 34-inch scale on the Precision (and later, the Jazz Bass). Fender *did* introduce a short-scale six-string bass guitar in the early '60s called the Bass VI (it even had a vibrato!), but their first four-string short-scale bass was a student model called the Mustang Bass, introduced in 1966.

The second electric bass introduced by Gibson was the EB-2, the bass variant of the semi-hollow series anchored by the ES-335. Introduced in 1958 along with the rest of the innovative semi-solids from Gibson, the EB-2 acquired a so-called push-button baritone switch (which simply changed the tone) the next year. The EB-2 ultimately became available in a two-pickup model (EB-2D), and was, along with a Gibson-made Epiphone clone called the Rivoli, a favorite of many original British Invasion bands in the mid-'60s. For example, it's been reported that the introductory bass riff to the Animals' "We Gotta Get Out of This Place" was played on such a model. This 1968 example is missing its pickguard.

EB-2, 1968. $700

46

The most successful basses for Gibson during the '60s "guitar boom" were the solidbody single-pickup EB-0, and its two-pickup sibling, the EB-3. The EB-0 was introduced in 1959, and had a slab-type body a la Les Paul Juniors and Specials of the same era, and featured a large pick-up mounted near the neck. The model would assume its classic SG shape in the early '60s, and also received a chrome pick-up cover. The EB-3 had a SG-shaped body from the outset (it was introduced in 1961—remember, Gibson's solidbody *guitar* lineup was also in transition at this time).

EB-0, 1960.
$2000

EB-0, 1965. $700

Handrests were found on many '60s EB-Os and EB-3s, and a cherry finish was standard for both models. EB-3s were most often associated with Jack Bruce, the bassist for the late '60s supergroup, Cream. When both models were offered in a 34½-inch scale variant, an "L" suffix was tacked onto the model numbers, and one version of the EB-0 had a built-in fuzztone (a distortion device), and was thus dubbed the EB-OF. Walnut finishes became available at the advent of the '70s, and a few rare natural finish EB-Os and EB-3s were made. The walnut-finish EB-3 seen here is an example of the short-lived slotted peghead variants. Unlike the rear-projecting banjo-style tuners seen on original Firebirds, the tuners on these basses were regular-style items that were simply mounted-on the side of the headstock, and strings were installed on extended posts in the slotted area. Why this design was supposed to be advantageous and/or innovative is anyone's guess.

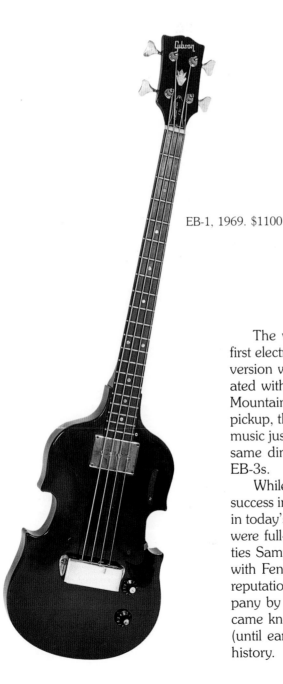

EB-1, 1969. $1100

EB-3, 1970. $850

The violin-shaped EB-1 seen here wasn't a re-issue of Gibson's first electric bass per se, but it did have the same body silhouette. This version was only around from about 1970 to 1972, and was associated with bassist Felix Pappalardi (now deceased) of the rock group Mountain ("Mississippi Queen"). Like other Gibson basses with a huge pickup, this bass had a booming, dark sound, which suited Mountain's music just fine, but curiously, the pickup on this EB-1 doesn't have the same dimensions as the similar-looking pickup seen on EB-Os and EB-3s.

While Gibson's short-scale basses garnered a nominal amount of success in their time, the 34-inch scale is now pretty much the standard in today's electric bass market. Subsequent basses proffered by Gibson were full-scale, but fared poorly, as the chapter titled "Sordid Seventies Samples and Early Eighties Oddities" will note. As was the case with Fender and CBS, the decline of Gibson's sales as well as their reputation for quality can be traced back to the acquisition of the company by an Equadorian company called ECL in late 1969. ECL became known as Norlin soon afterwards, and their time of ownership (until early 1986) is considered to be the darkest period in Gibson's history.

As of this writing, *Argentinosaurus huinculensis* ranks as the largest dinosaur that ever roamed the earth. While new discoveries about fossilized species happen on a regular basis (Giganotosaurus dethroned Tyrannosaurus Rex as the largest carnivore in the early '90s, for example), there doesn't seem to be any doubt that the Harmony company was the U.S. guitar equivalent of the giant herbivore that used to walk in the part of South America from whence it got its name. Like Argentinosaurus, American-made Harmony guitars are extinct.

In the halcyon days of American guitar manufacturing, Chicago was to fretted instruments what Detroit was to automobiles (and *that* scenario has also changed). Harmony led the pack regarding production totals for many years, claiming at one point to have been making more instruments than all other U.S. guitar manufacturers combined! The Harmony lineup during the '50s, '60s and early '70s consisted of its own moniker as a flagship, a sub-brand of acoustic guitars called Stella, and dozens of house brands. For most of their final quarter-century of existence, Harmony used cheap DeArmond pickups on their electric guitars and basses; such instruments were inexpensive and relatively durable. Players had a myriad of Harmony models from which to choose, particularly if house brands figured into the mix.

As noted in the "Progenitors" chapter, Harmony entered the solidbody electric guitar market with the H44 Stratotone in 1953. That model name would appear on other electrics throughout the decade, and into the next. The H42/1 Stratotone "Newport" shown here has the same silhouette as the H44, but its body is thinner (and it's bordered with *metal* binding, a la a kitchen dinette table of the same vintage). The single concentric control knob for volume and tone is a somewhat different-but-practical idea, and is all the more interesting because the volume control is the outer/larger (therefore easier-to-grip) knob.

H42/1 Stratotone-Newport, 1956. $200

The instruments on these two pages are examples of the Stratotone "planetary" series. Stratotones got a major makeover in 1958—their bodies were enlarged, and affected a silhouette that was even more like a single-cutaway Les Paul, but the new Stratotones were *hollow* (catalogs touted the instruments' "tone chamber" construction). Note that all examples still have an "atomic" logo on their headstocks.

The single-pickup H47 Mercury was hyped as having "triple pickup performance with a single unit" (it had a three-way "RHYTHM-TREBLE-BASS" switch). The H48 offered a natural-finish figured maple body with a tortoise-shell pickguard for $5.00 more (list price). Pickups on Mercury and Jupiter models were DeArmond "Golden Tone" units, but this H48 has what appears to be a fully-original DeArmond "toaster-top" pickup, which were often seen as add-on units that would "electrify" a flat-top acoustic guitar. Interestingly, the H47 was also available in a left-handed edition at one time (unusual for a budget instrument) for an upcharge of $18.00.

H47 Stratotone-Mercury, ca. 1960. $200

H48 Stratotone-Mercury, 1960. $225

The cheapest "planetary" Stratotones were the H45 and H46 Mars models shown at the left on the next page, which had dot markers and smaller headstocks. The "atomic" logo on the pickguard apparently did not appear until the latter portion of the models' existence. Like earlier single-pickup Stratotones (Mercury models excepted), the H45 had a tone bypass switch. The H46 offered a second pickup, a toggle switch, and concentric volume/tone knobs for about $25.00 more.

H45 Stratotone-Mars,
ca. 1960. $175

Just as Jupiter is the largest planet in the solar system, the H49 Jupiter was the ultimate model of the Stratotone "planetary" series. It featured a conventional three-way switch, separate volume and tone controls for each pickup, and an unusual "blender" knob. One unusual construction feature of the H49 was its spruce top. Again, the tortoise-shell pickguard (albeit somewhat long and narrow) is an oh-so-cool part of this top-of-the-line Stratotone. Its price in a 1963 catalog was $149.50.

H49 Stratotone-Jupiter,
ca. 1960. $250

H46 Stratotone-
Mars, ca. 1963.
$200

During the Golden Age of American-made electric guitars, Harmony produced a generous amount of hollowbody electric models—some full-depth, some thinline. Many of them appeared to have been inspired by higher-end (and more costly) competitors' models, yet some of the Harmony models had their own commendable innovations. As a nod to the Chicago behemoth's mass production, all of the instruments shown in this genre have bolt-on necks. Check out the differences in f-holes on these examples, as well.

The Meteor could easily have been dubbed a "poor man's Byrdland." It had the same shallow body depth, single-cutaway profile, and control layout as Gibson's frontline thinline electric, and the natural-finished H-71 seen here has a laminated spruce top (the Byrdland had a *carved* spruce top). The sunburst H-70 has a laminated maple top, as did Gibson's ES-350T/ES-350TD. Note the different pickups on these two Meteors, as well as the slightly-dissimilar tailpieces.

H71 Meteor, 1959.
$400

H70 Meteor, 1965.
$375

H76, 1965.
$475

In spite of its visual similarity to Gibson ES-335s and Guild Starfires, the Harmony H-76 may well have been America's most versatile electric guitar (and the same could be said for its equivalent house brands). A fully-hollow model, the H-76 was the top of the line electric guitar for Harmony, fully dressed with three pickups, multiple binding, and a maple body (the attractive light sunburst finish is similar to Gibson's "ice tea" sunburst of the same time period). It not only had a tortoise-shell pickguard, but a way-cool fully-laminated tortoise-shell headstock (including the truss rod cover) with the Harmony logo and fleur-de-lis decoration routed into the plastic, and an oval-shaped tortoise-shell pickup toggle switch plate as well. The H76's "versatility champ" designation comes from the fact that each pickup has a separate off-on switch, allowing for a total of seven different sounds instantly (individual pickups or any combination). Each pickup also has its own volume and tone control. The Bigsby vibrato tops off the sonic capabilities of the H76, and it also figures into the model number; the non-vibrato version of this instrument was the H75. In fact, a 1965 Harmony catalog shows the H75 and a red-tinted fraternal twin (the H77) and not only trumpets the instrument's "maximum electronics," the Bigsby-equipped variants are cited as being available by special order.

The least-fancy Harmony hollowbody electrics were found in the redoubtable Rocket series. Rockets were available in several different configurations, but perhaps the most unusual variant was the three-pickup H59. Unlike the H76, et. al., the H59's pickup capabilities were limited—note the "1-2-3-ALL" pickup settings for the four-position rotary switch on the treble cutaway. While the Gibson's high-end jazz box, the ES-5 Switchmaster, had the same type of pickup selection, the Switchmaster was a full-depth instrument, while the H59 was a thinline. At least the H59 has separate volume and tone controls each pickup; note how the knobs are lined up around the lower bout of the body. This example's pickguard has been signed by rock guitarists Ted Nugent and Mick Ralphs (and that's a backstage pass from a 1995 Nugent/Bad Company tour stuck in the strings). The "concept" of autographed guitars is somewhat nebulous within the collectible instrument market—some dealers specialize in such items, but insist on authenticity; ideally, a photo of a "celebrity" signing a particular instrument should be available. Then there's the question of how much a celebrity's signature increases the value of an instrument, how much of a "celebrity" a signatory happens to be, and even whether or not the signatory is deceased. One dealer specializing in autographed memorabilia has opined that an instrument with one celebrity's autograph is worth more than one with numerous signatures.

H72, 1966.
$300

H59 Rocket, 1964. Autographed guitar, $?

As the "guitar boom" of the '60s mushroomed, Harmony's new introductions affected a few more modern aesthetic features, as exemplified by the 1966 H72 seen here. Note the Fenderish headstock in particular—this guitar dates from the same year that Fender's Coronado hollowbody electric instruments were introduced, which could make for some interesting speculation about the guitar manufacturing industry's trends back then. This H72 also has unusual f-holes and updated control knobs.

The H79 12-string electric had the same body as the H72, and its harp-shaped tailpiece had appeared earlier as a six-string type on other Harmony instruments. Its headstock's outline is vaguely reminiscent of a Rickenbacker 12-string guitar's headstock, but unlike a Rick's innovative tuner layout, this guitar simply has standard tuners (with extended posts) attached to the sides of its headstock (Re: the Gibson EB-3 bass seen in the "Standards" chapter).

H79, 1967. $350

H14 Silhouette, 1966.
Autographed guitar, $?

H15V Silhouette, 1967.
$200

Harmony returned to the true solidbody electric guitar market in 1962, with the introduction of its new "Silhouette" series, which had solid maple bodies with a Jazzmaster-style offset profile. Most models were finished in a two-tone black-and-yellow sunburst, as seen on the two examples here. The pickguard on the single-pickup H14 has been signed by Roy Clark, and the instrument continues the tradition of a tone bypass switch on Harmony's one-pickup "starter" guitars; factory literature describes the Hl4's flippable gizmo as a "slider switch for quick change rhythm to take-off." The H15V was the two-pickup Silhouette with Harmony's own no-frills vibrato.

One of the most unusual series of Harmony instruments from the Golden Age of American electric guitars was the "Rebel" aggregation, introduced in the late '60s. The H81 (one-pickup), H82, and H82G seemed to have been influenced by several classic models from other manufacturers, but they also had some of their own unique attributes. The body in this series of guitars resembles certain Rickenbackers—it's hollow, has offset pointed cutaways and an unusual soundhole, and is bound front and rear. The headstock has a Fender-ish shape, but the oversize white truss rod cover looks almost exactly the same as the part that was found on the headstocks of Gibson Firebirds! Rebels had separate off/on slider switches for each pickup, and their volume and tone controls were slider-type as well; factory literature referred to this setup as "Stick-Shift Controls." As the '60s wore on, Harmony began to use parts from overseas suppliers, and the bridges on the Rebel series appear to have been imported.

H82G Rebel, 1972.
Autographed guitar, $?

H82 Rebel, 1969. $275

And guess what the 'G' stands for in this H82G's model number? This hideous avocado-to-black sunburst (perhaps inspired by the home appliance market around the same time this guitar was made) seemed to be an exclusive Harmony color ... and for good reason! The upper portion of the two-piece pickguard has been signed by Mark Farner, Mel Schacher, and Don Brewer, the three members of Grand Funk Railroad, which reunited in 1996 and toured for approximately three years. That's another backstage pass in the strings...is anybody starting to notice a trend here?

As improbable as it may sound, Harmony waited a full decade after the debut of the Fender Precision to enter the electric bass market their first low-end instrument was announced in a 1961 catalog. The H22 was a short-scale, hollowbody bass with a single cutaway (it later switched to a double-cutaway body style). Distinguishing (or dubious) features included a headstock with regular-size tuning keys (instead of larger tuners specifically designed for basses), a two-position rotary tone switch, a thumbrest *and* a fingerrest (at opposing angles), and an outlandish (and ultimately endearing?) pickguard—when viewed vertically, the large, angular piece of white plastic *seems* to resemble an angelfish; when viewed horizontally, a B-2 Stealth Bomber comes to mind. H22s were lightweight and easy to play, and that huge pickguard added a modicum of snazziness (or gaudiness, depending on your point of view). The signatories on this example are Billy F Gibbons, Dusty Hill, and Frank Beard of ZZ TOP, as well as the King of the Blues, B.B. King (Mr. King's autograph is in blue ink, of course).

H22, 1972.
Autographed bass,
$?

H27, 1967.
$475

The not-often-seen H-27 bass was apparently supposed to be the upscale companion to instruments such as the H75 and H76, and this example's cosmetic features seem to aver such a presumption. Its somewhat-oversized Fenderish headstock is completely laminated in tortoise-shell (including, once again, the truss rod cover), but the Harmony logo on this instrument is a piece of metal script that is attached to the laminate. While there's no pickguard, the toggle switch plate, thumbrest, and fingerrest are also "tortoise-topped." The knobs are the more-modern style, and the body's light sunburst finish allows a nominal amount of figured maple "flame" to be seen. Like a lot of hollowbody instruments (particularly basses) this H27 is somewhat "neck-heavy;" it feels quite unbalanced to a musician playing it in a standing position. Nevertheless, this instrument, like other upgrade Harmony products, seems to be offering a mixture of class and aesthetically unique features at an affordable price. Such a "pitch" was probably implicit when the instrument was new, and it's also applicable to the H27's status as a vintage instrument.

56

Harmony made dozens of private label brands for retailers, distributors, and other businesses for decades. Many times, their house brand instruments were based on Harmony's own models, with a few cosmetic differences. As Sears was the nation's biggest retailer during Harmony's heyday, the two giants in their respective fields had an ongoing business relationship for decades (and Sears actually owned Harmony at one time); there's no telling how many instruments made by Harmony had the Silvertone logo on their headstocks.

This full-depth, black jazz box was in the Sears catalog for many years. Its catalog designation in the '50s was the 01385L, and in the Spring 1960 catalog its model number changed to 1427L. Some versions of this model had aluminum binding on the front and back, as seen on the mid-'50s H42/1 Stratotone Newport earlier.

Silvertone 01385L,
1950s. $400

Silvertone 1423L,
early 1960s. $250

Silvertone 1477L,
mid-60s. $200

Another popular Silvertone-by-Harmony model was the 1423L, which was introduced after Harmony's own hollow "tone chamber" Stratotones hit the market (the earliest appearance of a Silvertone variant of a hollow Stratotone was the 01326L's debut in the Spring/Summer 1959 Sears catalog). The 1423L was an obvious fraternal twin of the H49 Jupiter, right down to the fifth knob, advertised in Sears' catalog as a "special-effects blender switch." Cosmetic differences included a black finish with a gold glitter effect, different pickup covers, and a "worm"-shaped control plate.

Another successful Silvertone model was the 1477L, a variant of the Silhouette H15V. Notice, however, that the pickups are perpendicular to the neck on the Silvertone model, whereas on the Harmony version, the pickups were set at an angle.

Harmony acquired the rights to the Regal brand name in the '50s (Regal had been a large manufacturer of budget instruments in the first half of the century), and opted to manufacture instruments with that brand to sell under alternative distribution arrangements. It's obvious that this Regal instrument is based on a "tone chamber" Stratotone (its internal production code indicates that it was known as the H265), but it has a highly unusual, very short 21½-inch scale. The reason such an instrument was made and marketed is unknown (for now).

Regal H265, 1959. $275

Sharp-eyed observers may note that the final house brand instrument shown is merely a black-and-glitter version of the single-pickup H45, and they're right (it even sports the latter-day "atomic" logo on its pickguard). The 'A' inside a tulip-like logo indicates that this instrument was marketed by the Alden's department store chain, which (like Harmony) is now out of business.

Harmony managed to lurch along a bit longer than some other U.S. budget guitar makers, finally closing its doors in 1976. Even the largest behemoth met with eventual extinction, but there are still a proportionately decent amount of vintage Harmonys out there (as well there should be!).

Alden's, early 1960s. $175

KAY: THE SEISMOSAURUS OF CHICAGO

Yep, as of this writing, the Seismosaurus is thought to have been the *second-largest* dinosaur that ever existed...

If Gibson and Fender were "the Big Two" of electric guitar history in the latter half of the 20th Century, Harmony and Kay were surely "the Big Two" of *budget* electric guitars of the early portion of the same half-century. Kay, like Harmony, was a Windy City manufacturing giant that made its own brand of instruments and a plethora of house brands. There are even some reports that Kay actually made more instruments *per day* at one time during the '60s "guitar boom", but Harmony ultimately outlasted the Kay company by about eight years.

Another parallel between the two Chicago companies was the fact that their roots each dated back to the late 1800s. The company that would become known as the Kay Musical Instrument Company in 1931 was originally known as the Groehsl Company, and became the Stromberg-Voisinet Company in the early '20s. Stromberg-Voisinet has a peculiar place in the pantheon of electric guitar lore, as in the late '20s, the company advertised a series of "Electro" instruments, including an electric guitar. By the '40s, Kay was already making house brand instruments. A Sears Silvertone outfit that included a Kay-made archtop electric Spanish guitar, amplifier, pick and instruction book was priced at $129.00 for the complete set in a 1946 catalog. Like most Kay electrics guitars of that era, the guitar that was proffered as catalog item #1323 had volume and tone controls located on the upper bass-side bout, near the neck joint.

The necks on Kay guitars tended to be quite chunky. One wag noted that if thick necks on other brands of instruments felt like two-by-fours, the necks on Kay guitars felt like two-by-sixes! When the company began concentrating on a variety of electrics in the early '50s, many of the cosmetic features of their instruments were probably considered "sharp" in their time, but one era's "sharp looks" can be another era's "endearing tackiness" (especially in the collectibles field). To wit:

The K-161 "Thin Twin" debuted in the early '50s, and has become known as the "Jimmy Reed model" due to its association with the legendary bluesman. It had a type of semi-solid construction (with a center block inside the body) that preceded Gibson's fabled ES-335 by several years, but it's possible that the block's main function was to support the pickups' huge magnets. The K-161 also had a flat top and back, and lacked soundholes. Pickguards (through which controls were loaded, and through which the pickups' blades protruded) were seen in all sorts of wildly-patterned tortoise-shell designs, and the natural-finish variant of the K-161 occasionally exhibited some moderate figuring. The headstock sports a hoity-toity crest that includes a lightning bolt, adding to the egregious gaucheness of this instrument.

K-161 Thin Twin, early 1950s. $350

The diminutive Pro appeared in 1954, and owed a lot of its styling to a Les Paul, but, it too had the same type of center-block construction as the K-161. The model was only available for three years, after which it morphed into the lowest-priced model in Kay's new "Gold 'K' Line," endorsed by award-winning jazz guitarist Barney Kessel (it appears that Kessel never actually played the Kay instruments bearing his name, and he subsequently went on to an endorsement model made by Gibson). Differences in the original Pro and the Barney Kessel Pro included pickups plus some cosmetic changes, the most obvious of which was the headstock. This keystone-shaped oversized peghead has been dubbed the "Kelvinator" headstock by vintage guitar enthusiasts, as the "K" on looks like the appliance manufacturer's logo. Moreover, the plastic overlay on the peghead has occasionally had the term "luncheonette" associated with it, as it appears to have been lifted from a counter top...

K172-S Pro, mid 1950s. $600

1701B Barney Kessel Pro, late 1950s. $700

K5965 Pro Bass, ca. 1960. $400

Unlike Harmony, Kay jumped on the electric bass bandwagon in the '50s, once it became apparent that the new instrument marketed by Fender wasn't a fluke. The first Kay bass was the Pro, introduced around the same time as the Pro guitar. Unlike its six-string companion, however, the Pro bass had a blade-type pickup a la the K-161 Thin Twin. Interestingly, the fretboards of many early Kay basses, including the Pro, didn't have position markers, but some models had markers on the side of the neck.

Kay jumped on another instrument bandwagon, that of the solidbody electric guitar, in the early '50s, around the same time as Gibson and Harmony. However, the surge in demand for student/budget instruments in the '60s prompted Kay to gear up for a massive increase in their mass production capacity, and the company also switched to a bolt-on neck design for almost all of their models, which boosted the quantity of instruments produced even more. A number of different body styles were created, and some of the headstock shapes contributed terms such as "bush axe" and "duck's bill" to the guitar lovers' lexicon. As Kay's production totals mushroomed, the quality of their instruments declined, but many, many aspiring guitarists learned to play on such cheap-if-uninspiring instruments.

Most likely, no other Kay model sums up that guitar manufacturer's place in guitar history better than a Vanguard. There's no telling how many thousands of these homely, no-frills guitars were cranked out by Kay during the '60s "guitar boom". Vanguards represented the epitome (or nadir, depending one's point of view) of the mass-produced, inexpensive American-made solidbody electric guitar. When they premiered in Kay's 1961 catalog, the single-pickup K100 listed for $59.95, and the two-pickup K102 listed for $79.95. From the headstock down, the paucity of cosmetic amenities is resounding: The logo on the headstock is simply a tin plate that's tacked on at two points, and a third attachment point also serves as the top hole for the bell-shaped truss rod cover. The fretboard has a grand total of *four* dot-shaped position markers, as well as *brass* frets. The pickups are flat and non-adjustable (and they usually sound pretty anemic). Mercifully, the bridge/tailpiece cover obscures a dinky, primitive-looking wood bridge. For some unknown reason, most (if not all) Vanguards have their volume and tone controls set up in a reverse configuration from the standard layout; i.e., the volume control is closer to the jack.

K100 Vanguard, mid 1960s.
$175

K102 Vanguard, mid 1960s.
$200

The "Value Leader" series consisted of one-, two-, and three-pickup guitars, and while they may have looked a bit classier than Vanguards, they still had their share of problems, particularly when it came to their aesthetics. The fretboard is hard rock maple, with tortoise-shell inlay (?), the bound hollow body is made of laminated maple, and unfortunately, the cheesy bridge on this series is exposed. Of special note is the pickguard, which is a textured metal trapezoid, touted in Kay catalogs as "an exclusive design." In the case of the two- and three-pickup Value Leader models, the rotary pickup selector is located next to the jack; since the guitar cord plugged in at a right angle, manipulating the pickup selector proved to be quite cumbersome for many players. Here's a ca. 1964 #K1962 example.

K1962, ca. 1964.
$250

K6535, mid 1960s. $200

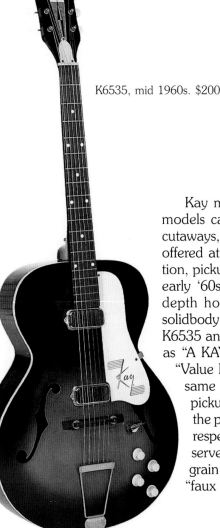

Kay made their share of hollowbody electrics, of course, and such models came in thinline or full-body configurations, with and without cutaways, and with one, two, or three pickups. Hollowbody electrics were offered at all sorts of price points, depending on their type of construction, pickups, etc. An interesting parallel could be found in some of Kay's early '60s catalogs, as the Chicago manufacturer offered a pair of full-depth hollowbody electrics at the same price point as the "starter" solidbody series, the aforementioned Vanguards. In fact, the two-pickup K6535 and the one-pickup K6533 were hyped in the first half of the '60s as "A KAY VALUE LEADER" in such catalogs, but weren't part of the "Value Leader" series noted previously. Instead, they appeared on the same page as the Vanguards, at similar prices—$59.95 for a one-pickup guitar; $79.95 for a two-pickup model (by the 1965 catalog, the price on the hollowbody electrics had risen to $64.50 and $85.00, respectively, while the Vanguards held their price). Sharp-eyed observers may note what appears to be some fairly spectacular wood grain on the sides of this K6535's body, but don't be impressed—it's "faux figuring," affected by spray paint. Now *that's* cheap!

As the Kay company began its downward spiral in the mid-'60s, new introductions by the company were not only uninspiring, they suffered from poor quality in their construction as well. One latter-day solidbody, the K355 Titan II, is exemplary (and quite enough to ponder). It doesn't look like anything special or innovative (and that was probably the opinion of players in the mid-'60s), and while it does have a "bush axe" headstock, its fretboard inlay looks like a half-hearted rip-off of the Gibson ES-175's fret markers, and the control knobs are a bit too close to each other to allow comfortable and dependable manipulation. Small wonder Kay was already in trouble when this guitar was introduced.

Old Kraftsman, 1950s.
$350

K355 Titan II, mid 1960s. $200

Old Kraftsman, 1960s.
$175

The two instruments seen on the left may look familiar, but a close scrutinization reveals that the headstocks of what appear to be a K-161 Thin Twin and a K-100 Vanguard are actually Old Kraftsman (Spiegel) house brand instruments. Other than the logos, there really isn't any difference between these instruments and their Kay brand clones.

The Old Kraftsman bass seen here is a twin of the Kay K5920 bass of the same vintage. Note the hollow archtop body with a single segmented f-hole and a Florentine cutaway; this body style was found on a lot of Kay instruments in the '60s.

The Truetone (Western Auto house brand) bass is a clone of the Kay 5915 bass, and dates from around the same time as the Old Kraftsman bass, but it has a hollow, flat body not unlike the #1962 Value Leader seen earlier. In what seems to be a *terrible* case of bungled marketing, neither one of these basses has fretboard markers or side dot markers! One would think a student player would have needed all the help he/she could get, including *visual* assistance, when learning to play, but these budget instruments don't offer any reference points anywhere on their necks. Both instruments also have a single chrome pickup with a "ridge" running lengthwise; sometimes this is referred to as a "Kleenex box" pickup due to its shape. Other aesthetic specialties for the Truetone include checkered binding, and an autograph from Who bassist John Entwhistle.

For whatever it was worth, a slightly-more-modernistic silhouette is seen on this Custom Kraft guitar. Custom Kraft was the house brand of St. Louis Music, a large wholesale distributor that is still in business as of this writing. This instrument was obviously inspired by the Gibson SG, but it actually bears a closer resemblance to a '70s Guild S-100 (the cutaways are more offset than an SG's). However, the also-apparently-SG-inspired Guild guitar didn't appear until two years after Kay had gone out of business. The decorations on the pickups and bridge/tailpiece cover are original (and note that the pickups and bridge/tailpiece cover are gold), but the neck still only has four fretboard markers and no side dot markers on its binding.

During its final throes as an American guitar manufacturer, Kay was owned by the Valco company, another Chicago instrument manufacturer with its own problems (see next chapter). Some instruments from those end times have parts from both companies, or switched around brand names (an originally-Valco-owned name such as Supro on an-originally-marketed-as-a-Kay product, for example). Locked in a fatal embrace/tailspin, what was left of two once-mighty Windy City builders crashed and burned in 1968.

Old Kraftsman bass, 1960s.
$300

Truetone bass, ca. 1965.
Autographed guitar, $?

Custom Kraft, 1960s.
$250

One of the animal kingdom's most oddball creatures (as anyone with a nominal interest in zoology probably already knows) is the platypus, a small mammal that looks like the result of a matter transference science experiment involving a duck and a beaver that went terribly awry. Platypi, also known as duckbills, not only have the type of snout and mouth from which they get their alternate name, they also have webbed feet and lay eggs. However, these unique animals also have fur and a wide, flat tail, and as noted earlier, nurse their young.

While Valco-made electric guitars were played pretty much like all other guitars, some of their bizarre aesthetics and construction features also resulted in such instruments garnering their fair share of terms in the glossary of the vintage guitar phenomenon—examples include "Gumby" headstocks, "Res-O-Glas" bodies, "Silversound" pickups, etc.

The roots of the Valco company date back to the National and Dobro companies of California, both of which were famous for their resonator acoustic guitars. After the two companies merged, the new organization moved to Chicago, where it ultimately became Valco Manufacturing Company in the early '40s. Its name was derived from the first letters of the given names of its founders, Victor Smith, Al Frost, and Louis Dopyera.

Like other Chicago manufacturers, Valco was primarily involved with budget instruments and house brands. Some of their electric instruments had relatively normal silhouettes, but others looked just plain weird (and perhaps that's what makes their odd-shaped guitars and basses the most desirable in the vintage guitar market).

The National nameplate was Valco's flagship brand, and perhaps these two black guitars are definitive examples of the company's unique instruments. The 1962 Val-Pro 88 and its successor, the Newport 88, both feature "map-shaped" bodies (note the differences in the two models) made of "Res-O-Glas," a type of molded Fiberglas (the two halves of the body snapped into a rubberized strip). While both guitars may look like they have too many control knobs, each has a third pickup, known as a "Silversound" unit, built into the bridge. Though quite innovative for their time, Silversound pickups were, um, "sonically-challenged" regarding their output.

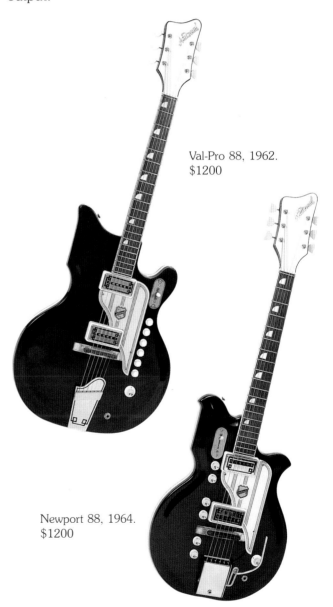

Val-Pro 88, 1962.
$1200

Newport 88, 1964.
$1200

Even National's thinlines offered a nominal amount of visual curiosities. The N830 was the lowest-priced thinline in National's final catalog in 1968, and has the ubiquitous "Gumby" headstock, bat-shaped f-holes, and a pickguard that looks like an elongated map of Australia when viewed horizontally. Its combination bridge/tailpiece unit is imported. The necks on such thinlines were bolt-on.

N830, 1968.
$350

N800 Bobbie Thomas, 1968. $400

Regionally-popular guitarist Bobbie Thomas would grace the front cover of the aforementioned final National catalog, along with a display of his signature series guitars, the top-of-the-line instruments for the company (an ultimately dubious distinction). The Bobbie Thomas Series came in three colors: "Sunset Orange" (N800), "Cherry Shade" (N801), and "Natural Blond" (N802). Catalog text cited the instruments' "Extra thick binding on all body edges and fingerboard" (the body edges have five layers, white-black-white-black-white). Note the bound f-holes, master volume control on the treble cutaway, and fancy fretboard inlay. The figuring on the maple bodies of these guitars is also attractive.

National Bobbie Thomas Series guitars were also the only guitars in the final catalog to display a top-grade Bigsby vibrato unit, but another interesting piece of hardware is the bridge—it's a Gibson ABR-1 model. In a 1990 interview, Thomas explained, "the Gibson ABR-1 was the standard bridge that came with the guitar. To the best of my recollection, it was chosen from the stock of available bridges at the time for its adjustability. It wasn't until sometime later that I learned it was a Gibson bridge."

N801 Bobbie
Thomas, 1968.
$400

N802 Bobbie
Thomas, 1968.
$400

Supro Super, 1961.
$300

Valco's "sub-brand" was known as Supro. In general, Supro guitars and basses were less-fancy and more "utilitarian" than National instruments, so more examples of this budget line probably found their way into the hands of neophyte players. The circa 1961 Supro Super shown here is a definitive example of an "entry level" Valco-made product, and its short 22-inch scale reinforces that notion.

The Supro Dual-Tone was one of the sub-brand's more popular offerings. It began as a wood-bodied instrument, and metamorphosed into a Res-O-Glas version in the early '60s. While its particular silhouette is a bit more, um, "traditional," it has a small "notch" on the bass-side of its upper bout, making it yet another visually-unique Valco item.

Supro Dual-Tone, early 1960s. $450

Supro Belmont, 1962. $400

The celluloid covering on this early '60s Supro Belmont has been nicknamed "mother of toilet seat" (a.k.a. "MOTS") within the vintage guitar collective. Its pearloid facade is usually found on pickguards, lap steels, and a few small amplifiers, but it's not surprising that Valco opted to apply it to some of their Spanish electric guitars as well.

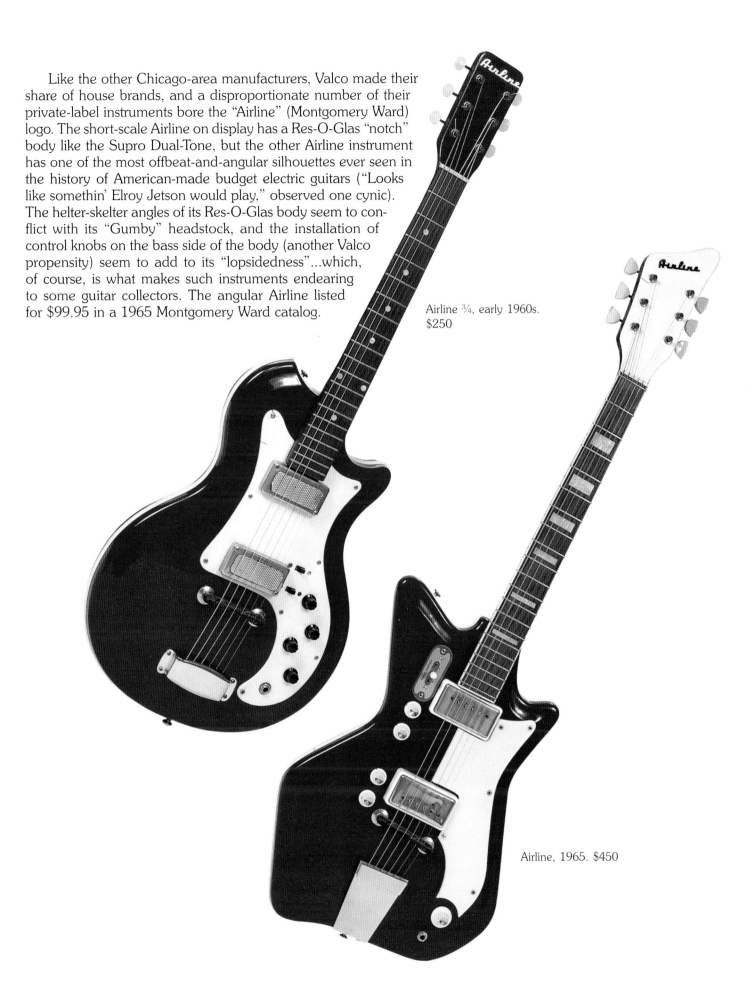

Like the other Chicago-area manufacturers, Valco made their share of house brands, and a disproportionate number of their private-label instruments bore the "Airline" (Montgomery Ward) logo. The short-scale Airline on display has a Res-O-Glas "notch" body like the Supro Dual-Tone, but the other Airline instrument has one of the most offbeat-and-angular silhouettes ever seen in the history of American-made budget electric guitars ("Looks like somethin' Elroy Jetson would play," observed one cynic). The helter-skelter angles of its Res-O-Glas body seem to conflict with its "Gumby" headstock, and the installation of control knobs on the bass side of the body (another Valco propensity) seem to add to its "lopsidedness"...which, of course, is what makes such instruments endearing to some guitar collectors. The angular Airline listed for $99.95 in a 1965 Montgomery Ward catalog.

Airline ¾, early 1960s.
$250

Airline, 1965. $450

Oahu brand guitars were marketed quite differently from other U.S. house brands (or National and Supro instruments, for that matter). The Oahu company primarily concerned itself with *mail order instruction courses* rather than selling musical instruments, and such courses tended to be oriented more towards Hawaiian/steel guitar players rather than Spanish guitar students. Regardless of which instrument a student chose, however, Oahu offered their own instruments as an option. An intriguing feature of this wood-bodied, short-scale Oahu guitar is its gold hardware, including gold Kluson tuners on the back of the headstock.

Oahu, 1959.
$400

Custom Kraft,
ca. 1967. $350

Last but not least, a Custom Kraft thinline electric seems to validate Valco's reputation as a manufacturer of wacky-looking guitars. It, too, dates from the company's final days, and while structurally similar to the National N830, its cosmetics include a "dragon snout" headstock, a slick-looking emerald-and-black shaded finish, an elevated pickguard on *both* sides of the body, and lightning bolt-shaped f-holes. The control knobs seem to have been stuck on wherever enough space could be found to install them.

As noted earlier, what was left of Valco went out of business along with what was left of Kay in 1968. Valco's Res-O-Glas instruments had been guaranteed not to fade or stain, but the company that made them did indeed fade away, leaving a somewhat different and dubious legacy.

And one wonders whether such Res-O-Glas instruments should be cleaned with Windex, or perhaps Corvette polish...

DANELECTRO: MOSTLY MASONITE

Nat Daniel's cheaply-made and cheaply-priced Danelectro instruments (and related house brands, particularly Sears' Silvertone moniker) rank among the all-time best-sellers in the history of American-made electric guitars. Their simple, practical, and/or endearing features (the latter adjective being more nostalgia-oriented) made them interesting to guitarists both then and now. Truckloads of instruments came rolling in out of the Danelectro factory in New Jersey during the decade and a half that the company made guitars (for the last couple of years of the manufacturer's existence, the company was owned by the giant MCA conglomerate).

The founder of Danelectro actually came up with more innovations in the electric guitar market (as well as amplifiers) than some enthusiasts may realize. Daniel had been making amplifiers since the 1930s, and began mass-producing amplifiers for Sears and Montgomery Ward at his Red Bank factory in the late '40s. Danelectro guitars debuted in 1954, as did Dano-made Silvertone instruments.

As Danelectro and Silvertone were always intertwined in the '50s and '60s (and at one point, says a former employee, 85 percent of the company's production volume bore the Sears nameplate), it seems appropriate that the earliest example seen here is indeed a Silvertone brand instrument. The 1377L had some intriguing facets in its construction, including an aluminum nut, a simple-and-somewhat-intonatable bridge/tailpiece unit, concentric volume and tone knobs, and pickups that are under raised areas on the Melamine pickguard. The body was made of solid poplar; note the exposed aluminum rod running through the middle.

Silvertone 1377L, ca. 1954.

The 1377L dispels the notion that Danelectro's fabled poplar-and-Masonite instruments were the first models introduced by the company, but those, er, "legendary" items didn't come along until 1956, when the "U" series was announced. In addition to a body made with a wood frame with a Masonite top and back, a stereotypical instrument had "lipstick tube" pickups, so named because that's exactly what they were—a supplier to the cosmetics industry also provided Danelectro with the housings for their pickups! The single-pickup "U-1" seen here has a Les Paul-shaped body with a "Coke bottle" headstock silhouette. Two- and three-pickup "U" series guitars were also made; they were known as the U-2 and the U-3—simple as that. The most popular colors in the series were copper and black.

U-1, 1956. $400

Silvertone 1373L, 1958. $650

While Fender's Precision Bass was, as previously noted, an entirely new and different type of instrument, Danelectro's first entry into the electric bass field was also unique, in that it was a *true* "bass guitar," sporting six strings tuned an octave below a standard guitar. It, too, hit the market in 1956; Fender and Gibson would not introduce similar instruments until several years later. The headstock of this late '50s Silvertone six-string bass is a slight variant of the Dano "Coke bottle" shape. Duane Eddy used such instruments on recordings such as "Because They're Young."

When Danelectro opted to introduce a more-in-line-with-the-marketplace four-string bass in late 1958, the new model also affected a double-cutaway body. This 3412 configuration was known as the "Shorthorn" body style, and was found on guitars as well (as popularized by Jimmy Page of Led Zeppelin). Note the "seal"-shaped pickguard.

3412, 1959.
$350

The circa 1964 Pro seen here was cosmetically befuddling. Introduced in '63, the Pro was the only Danelectro guitar with such a body and headstock shape (thank goodness; it's almost *too* oddball, even by Danelectro standards). Nevertheless, it was the first Dano instrument to have an innovative "tilt" control to allow an adjustment of the neck angle, using an Allen wrench... and it preceded Fender's similar construction feature by almost a decade (Tilt-neck Fender guitars and basses weren't highly regarded in the '70s, nor are they as highly-sought as most other Fenders in the used/vintage market). Danelectro ultimately incorporated their tilt-neck design into their entire lineup.

Pro, ca. 1964. $400

Here's an unusual participant in the "not-necessarily-acoustic" category. The Convertible was true to its name—it was available as an acoustic guitar (at a list price of $45 when it was introduced in 1959), but the acoustic variant featured pre-drilled holes, which were topped with "decorative inserts," according to one catalog. An optional $20 kit, consisting of a pickup and controls, would convert the instrument into an electric; the volume and tone controls and the jack were installed in the aforementioned pre-drilled holes (a fully-assembled electric Convertible was offered for $65). The same catalog ad asserted that "As a non-electric, this model produces clear sustained tones." Nonsense—it's got all of the tonal dynamics and bluesy sustain of a banjo, but it's still a cool item.

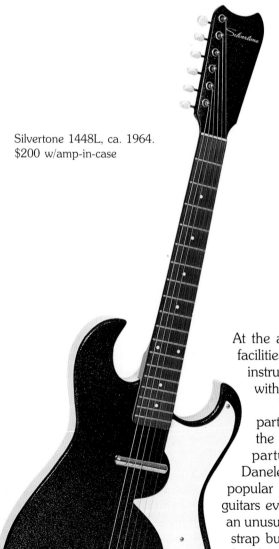

Silvertone 1448L, ca. 1964.
$200 w/amp-in-case

Convertible, early 1960s.
$450

At the advent of the '60s "guitar boom", Danelectro relocated their facilities to Neptune City, and it has been estimated that 150 to 200 instruments were made each day at the factory during such times, with most of them being shipped to a Sears warehouse.

While Danelectro brand guitars and their Silvertone counterparts had featured nearly-identical silhouettes from the beginning, the fabled Silvertone "amp-in-the-case" models represented a departure for the manufacturer, as there were no corresponding Danelectro models. These extremely affordable, therefore extremely popular instruments debuted in late 1962, and were probably the first guitars ever owned by many Baby Boomers. Their body silhouette had an unusual double-cutaway shape, with a slight indentation near the rear strap button (one wag stated that it reminded him of an apple). The headstock was also cosmetically unique, with six-on-a-side tuners running parallel to the neck, as well as a "scooped out" look near the logo.

The 1448L may be the all-time champ of American-made budget/student electric guitars. It came with an amplifier built into the carrying case and instructional items, and was priced at $67.95, complete.

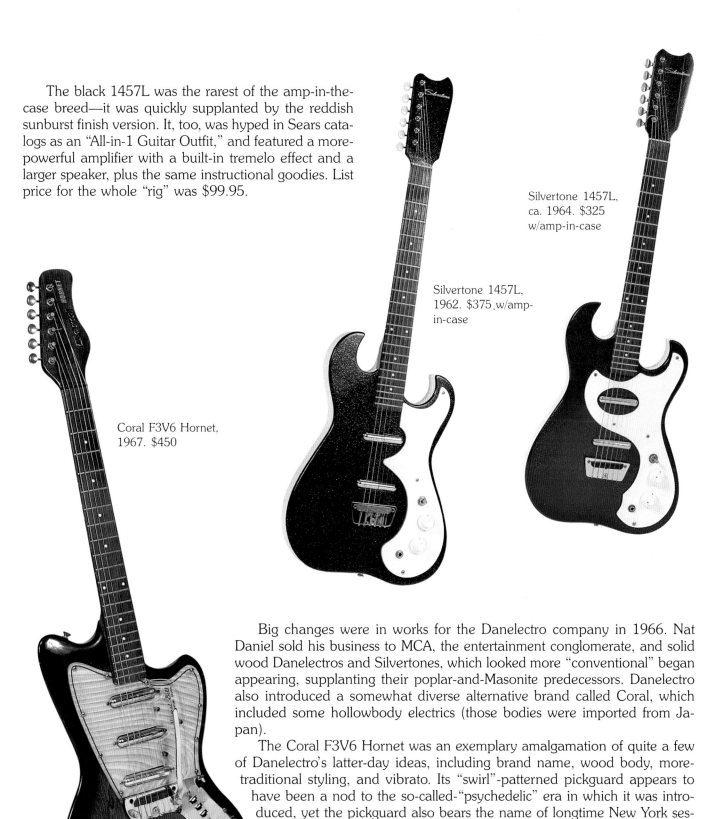

The black 1457L was the rarest of the amp-in-the-case breed—it was quickly supplanted by the reddish sunburst finish version. It, too, was hyped in Sears catalogs as an "All-in-1 Guitar Outfit," and featured a more-powerful amplifier with a built-in tremelo effect and a larger speaker, plus the same instructional goodies. List price for the whole "rig" was $99.95.

Silvertone 1457L,
ca. 1964. $325
w/amp-in-case

Silvertone 1457L,
1962. $375 w/amp-
in-case

Coral F3V6 Hornet,
1967. $450

Big changes were in works for the Danelectro company in 1966. Nat Daniel sold his business to MCA, the entertainment conglomerate, and solid wood Danelectros and Silvertones, which looked more "conventional" began appearing, supplanting their poplar-and-Masonite predecessors. Danelectro also introduced a somewhat diverse alternative brand called Coral, which included some hollowbody electrics (those bodies were imported from Japan).

The Coral F3V6 Hornet was an exemplary amalgamation of quite a few of Danelectro's latter-day ideas, including brand name, wood body, more-traditional styling, and vibrato. Its "swirl"-patterned pickguard appears to have been a nod to the so-called-"psychedelic" era in which it was introduced, yet the pickguard also bears the name of longtime New York session ace (and Danelectro endorser) Vincent Bell, which seems like a bit of a paradox ... note the individual off/on slider switches for each pickup.

MCA closed down Danelectro in 1968—as noted earlier, not a good year for the U.S. budget guitar manufacturing business.

GRETSCH: BIG GUITARS FROM THE BIG CITY

A stereotypical reaction when one hears the Gretsch brand name mentioned is to associate such guitars with legendary picker Chet Atkins. True, Atkins endorsed and played Gretsch guitars for many years, but the original New York-based company made many more models than the variants bearing the Chet Atkins moniker. The company has been through more than one owner, and Gretsch instruments have been made in more than one location. What's more, Chet Atkins became a Gibson endorser in 1981.

But it's the older Gretsch arch-top electrics, many of which are indeed Chet Atkins models, that command the most interest among vintage guitar aficionados. Quite frankly, the quality and workmanship on some New York-made Gretsch instruments is atrocious, so guitars and basses in this segment of the old guitar market should be examined closely on an individual basis, but there *are* some goods ones around.

Another term that is applicable to Gretsch electric instruments made in the Big Apple is "incongruous." The manufacturer was constantly making changes in its lineup's cosmetic and/or electronic features, so one will almost never hear the term "transitional" associated with Gretsch guitars and basses, because for all intents and purposes, they were *all* transitional.

The 1957 model 6190 Streamliner shown here is a good example of such ongoing changes. It sports the short-lived mid-'50s "hump block" fret inlay, and several of its parts would be replaced in the near future. The primitive-but-intonatable Melita bridge would be supplanted by a "Space Control" roller-type bridge, which allowed string spacing but didn't allow intonation (?); the DeArmond Dyna-Sonic pickup would be replaced by Gretsch's own Filter'Tron humbucking pickup (one legend has it that Gretsch parted ways with DeArmond because the pickup company cut a big deal with the gargantuan Harmony company), and "neo-classical" fretboard inlay took the place of the hump blocks. Most Streamliners had the term "Electromatic" etched into their headstocks (vertically), but this one doesn't.

6190 Streamliner, 1957. $1500

The model 6120 Chet Atkins instruments are, of course, considered primo rockabilly guitars, and the flagship endorsement model for Gretsch (introduced in 1954) had as many cosmetic and electronic variants as other Gretsches. This 1960 model has a lot of the right stuff—two Filter'Tron pickups, a Gretsch/Bigsby vibrato (the "V"-shaped cutout is exclusive to the Bigsbys found on Gretsches), and an ebony fretboard with neo-classical/"thumbprint" inlay. One can only wonder why the model came (at the time this guitar was made) with the simplest of bar-type bridges (non-intonatable, of course).

6120 Chet Atkins, 1960.
$3750

6120 Chet Atkins, 1965.
$2000

The 6120 was in for some big changes circa 1962. It assumed a double-cutaway profile with an "Electrotone" body that, while hollow, did not have any f-holes (the ones seen on it were painted on). The electronic "innards" of this model loaded through a hole in the rear of the body that was covered with a plastic lid and a large, snap-on vinyl pad that covered the lid. The transition of the name of this model from "6120" to "Nashville" in the mid-'60s is nebulous when it comes to the chronology; this '65 guitar doesn't have a nameplate on the headstock, nor a "Nashville" notation on the pickguard, so it's still a 6120 (of sorts).

It's easy to determine that this #6119 Chet Atkins Tennes-sean is a first-year model, as it has a standard Bigsby vibrato (Gretsch/Bigsby vibratos came along in 1959). The Tennessean went through a number of changes in its lifetime (including the acquisition of two pickups in the early '60s), but first-configura-tion examples like this one were the only notable Gretsch hollowbody electrics with a single pickup near the bridge (the Filter'Tron on this #6ll9 has "Patent Applied For" embossed on it). They were also the only Chet Atkins series Gretsches with a black pickguard.

6119 Tennessean, 1958.
$2000

The Anniversary series, celebrating Gretsch's 75th annum, debuted in 1958, and were available in not only single- and double-pickup models but unique two-tone colors as well. This 1964 model 6118 Double Anniversary is in a "Smoke Green" finish, but it also has anemic-sounding Hi-Lo-Tron pickups, which Anniversarys acquired at the advent of the '60s.

6118 Double Anniversary, 1964. $1200

6129 Silver Jet, 1956. $4500

Early Gretsch "solidbodies" weren't solid. They were built in a configuration that had hollow chambers inside, but the New York company certainly fostered the perception that they were following the lead of Gibson on more than one occasion. Aesthetically, the earliest examples of Gretsch's Jet series resembled Gibson's Les Paul, but to its credit, the Big Apple manufacturer offered more than one finish on such instruments. One of the coolest models was the model 6129 Silver Jet, topped by a piece of sparkle-finish Nitron (as found on drum shells). Note the two DeArmond pickups and Melita bridge on this 1956 example. One vintage dealer specializing in Gretsches reported that interest in the Silver Jet exploded after Aerosmith's Joe Perry was seen playing one in the video of "Dude Looks Like a Lady."

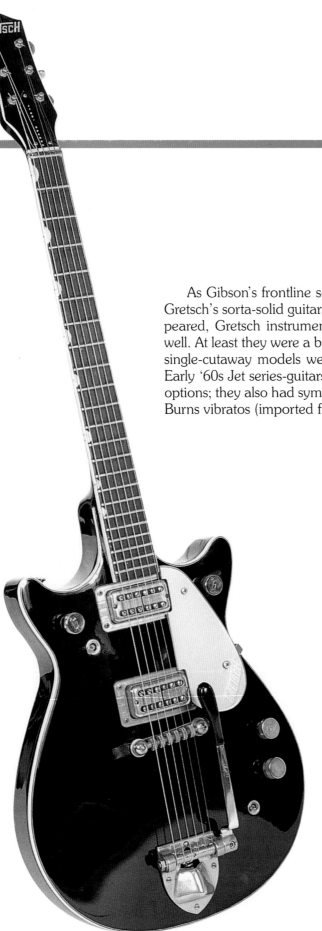

As Gibson's frontline solidbodies changed body styles, so did Gretsch's sorta-solid guitars; i.e., when Gibson's SG silhouette appeared, Gretsch instruments affected a double-cutaway style as well. At least they were a bit more different from SGs than original single-cutaway models were when compared to '50s Les Pauls. Early '60s Jet series-guitars still had bound tops and several color options; they also had symmetrical cutaways. Some examples had Burns vibratos (imported from England), as seen on this Duo-Jet.

6128 Duo-Jet, 1963.
$1500

And what in the world was Gretsch trying to accomplish or prove with the model 6126 Astro-Jet? It looks like a lop-sided Gibson SG, and its unusual 4 + 2 headstock is unique to the model (and also looks like it's melted). It also has Super-'Tron pickups, which have exposed bars instead of polepieces. The Astro-Jet was only in Gretsch's lineup for about three years in the mid-'60s.

6126 Astro-Jet, 1966.
$700

6132 Corvette, 1965.
$450

While Gretsch never really pursued the student guitar market—at least, not *publicly*—the company *did* offer some relatively no-frills, "semi-budget" guitars, priced below the frontline Jet series. Debuting in the early '60s, the Corvette series was apparently an attempt to compete with instruments such as Gibson's SG Specials and Juniors...and they looked a lot like their competitors. However, Corvettes had Hi-Lo 'Tron pickups, which weren't even in the same sonic ballpark as Gibson's potent P-90s. The series was offered in one- or two-pickup models; vibratos (mostly Burns) were also available. A few rare colorful variants, such as the Princess and the Twist (which had a candy-striped pickguard) were also made. Originally, Corvettes had a standard 3 + 3 headstock shape, but a unique "quasi-reverse Fender" shape showed up in 1965. The 'Vettes were vanquished by the end of the decade in which they premiered.

The final New York-made Gretsch on display simply re-affirms the utter unpredictability of this brand's models. The Monkees endorsement model is unique enough in Gretsch lore—it's the only model ever to have double-thumbprint/neo-classical fret markers, not to mention the fact that the band that gave it its name had a minimal amount of musical talent (some cynics dubbed the Monkees the "Pre-Fab Four"). The Gretsch Monkees model also had Super-'Tron pickups and real f-holes, and was presented as having a V-cutout Gretsch/Bigsby vibrato. However, this example has what appears to be an original Burns vibrato—go figure. The Monkees model was never catalogued, and was only around for a couple of years...just like the Monkees' TV show.

Monkees Rock n' Roll, 1966. $1500

7576 Country Club, 1980. $1400

This attractive Country Club model (note the grain on the body) wasn't made in New York—it's of 1980 vintage. It demonstrates that while most of the Baldwin-era, Arkansas-made Gretsch products tend to be maligned (and avoided) by many guitar collectors (see "Sordid Seventies Samples and Early-Eighties Oddities" for more than one example), some decent and high-quality instruments were made by Gretsch during that turbulent time in its history. In fact, some of the Arkansas higher-end Gretsch products were superior to their New York counterparts—in the opinion of more than one Gretsch aficionado—which, of course, doesn't make the Arkansas-made guitar more valuable than the New York-made guitar, but the craftsmanship on this Country Club is quite good. Many Baldwin-era Gretsches have a squared-off pickguard as seen here, and the smoked see-through tint of the pickguard and the tailpiece inset add a moderate amount of "coolness" to the instrument.

360F, 1960.
$2000

Contrary to stereotyping, Fender wasn't the only legendary electric guitar brand that was born and bred in the Golden State. Two other notable companies have made quality instruments in California for decades. One of 'em markets their guitars and basses in a unique way, and a third fabled builder had its genesis on the Left Coast, but has been made in several different states (and its current status is unclear as of this writing).

RICKENBACKER

Rickenbacker instruments have definitely carved out their own niche in the guitar market. The company made some of the first commercially-viable electric guitars (Hawaiian and Spanish) in the 1930s, but the brand's status among players mushroomed in the '60s, thanks to use by such bands as the Beatles and the Byrds. Under the aegis of F.C. Hall (1909-1999), whose Radio-Tel company in Santa Ana had been the exclusive distributor for the earliest Fender guitars and amplifiers, Rickenbacker guitars and basses offered some brilliant innovations and alternative sounds to '60s players who were most likely oriented towards Gibson and Fender products.

All of the '60s Ricks seen here have what are usually termed "chrome bar" pickups. They closely resemble DeArmond "toaster top" units, but were Rickenbacker-made.

The earliest Rickenbacker seen here is also one of the rarest. The "F" series had a thinline, single-cutaway style and was made from the late '50s to the early '70s. This 1960 360F has Rickenbacker's "Deluxe" features—triangle-shaped inlay, neck and body binding, etc., and on this example, the body binding is checkered. It has an early variant of Rickenbacker's "Fireglo" sunburst finish (the yellowish portion would ultimately assume a more pinkish tinge), and "TV" or "stovetop" control knobs (so named because they look like they are better-suited for placement on an appliance instead of a guitar). This example also has a replacement "R" tailpiece, which Rickenbacker introduced later in the '60s.

One of Rickenbacker's most enduring designs is the series that consisted of double-cutaway, thinline hollowbodies with Deluxe features (the 360, 365, 370, and 375). The two-pickup, non-vibrato 360 is still in production, but the top-of-the-line 375 had roughly the same chronology as the aforementioned "F" series (a variant of the 375 was re-issued from 1984-1990). The series to which the 375 belonged started out with a body that was bound front and rear, and cutaways that were more pointed. Such models assumed the "softer" profile seen here (rounded top with no binding, rounder cutaways) in the mid-'60s.

375, 1967.
$1400

330-12, 1967.
$1400

It's quite possible that Rickenbacker's most important legacy in the electric guitar phenomenon was the development of guitars that have ultimately become standard for electric 12-string instruments. Rick's innovative string layout and the utterly unique tuning gear/headstock design turned the industry on its ear in the mid-'60s, as did the instruments' inimitable sound—the Byrds' "Mr. Tambourine Man" is a definitive example. The series that included the 330-12 shown here had "Standard" features (plainer body, dot markers, no binding). But it's that headstock that gets a viewer's attention...

Rickenbacker's efforts in solidbody guitars weren't as innovative, but their instruments were and are high-quality items—this 625 is every bit as nice as the company's hollowbody electrics, even though the hollowbody models were and are more popular.

625, 1965.
$1000

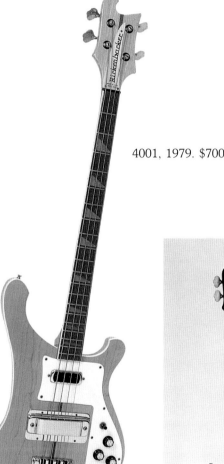

4001, 1979. $700

4005, 1979.
$1200

Rickenbacker International Corporation C.E.O. John Hall (son of F.C. Hall) was questioned in a 1993 interview about a Rickenbacker bass sound having its own "niche" and he responded: "It very definitely does; you'd have to call it a 'high-fidelity bass' sound." When introduced in the '50s, Rickenbacker's solidbody bass differed radically from Fender's regarding its looks *and* sound. Its flowing, "cresting wave" body silhouette was artistic and elegant, and its neck-through construction tends to evoke an almost piano-like tone. Rick basses have been refined, of course, but they still look a lot like they did when they hit the market. Rickenbacker's success story in the bass market is the reverse of its success in the guitar market; i.e., their solidbody models have always been more popular than their hollowbody basses (but either style has its own panache).

MOSRITE

The saga of the Mosrite company is the antithesis of that of Rickenbacker. While the Hall family's enterprise has remained in Orange County, California for decades, the production facilities of Mosrite were somewhat like a migratory mushroom—the company would pop up in one location, close its doors, then appear somewhere else. It's been reported that Mosrite guitars were made in North Carolina, Nevada, Arkansas, and more than one town in California, where Semie Moseley (1935-1992) got his start in the '50s.

The Ventures and Mosrite guitars are probably the first "band/brand" association that most aging Boomers who aspired to be guitarists recall from the '60s "guitar boom". The Mosrite solidbody that ultimately attained the instrumental combo's endorsement had a body silhouette that looked like a "reverse Stratocaster" (longer cutaway horn on the treble side). Mosrite guitars usually had a vibrato with feather-light manipulation, and were highly desirable to teen-age players during the '60s. It's ironic that the Ventures' association with Mosrite only lasted about five years during that decade; they played Fender instruments before and after their Mosrite endorsement years.

The Mosrite Ventures model bass seen here is, according to Ventures bassist Bob Bogle, possibly one-of-a-kind. It has the stereotypical Mosrite body silhouette and "German carve" on its top, "duckfoot" tuners, and a super-thin neck on a 30-inch scale. However, the logo and brand name on the pickguard are unique—Bogle recalls that the company made a set of instruments for the Ventures with such inlay, since the headstock's logo and model name are hard to see. The pickguard inlay showed up better on television, so if there ever was a Mosrite that deserved a "TV model" designation (albeit unofficial), this bass would be a rare example of such (at last report, it was due to be put on display in a Hard Rock Cafe).

Mosrite's other instruments also proffered some unique innovations and/or aesthetics. The Mark X (Roman numeral "ten") bass seen here was part of the series that was, according to a '60s catalog, "...inspired by the spirited flying fingers of Joe Maphis," a talented Western music guitarist. Its walnut back and sides were actually hollowed out of three pieces of wood that were glued together then routed out; i.e., there's no rear binding, because the back and sides aren't separate pieces. The spruce top also has a German carve, but lacks f-holes, even though the body is a semi-hollow style.

Ventures model, 1965. Probably one-of-a-kind, $?

Joe Maphis/Mark X, mid-1960s. $1000

86

The Combo had the same body silhouette as the Maphis model, but also had an f-hole and a flat back (necessitating rear binding). In the aforementioned catalog, a similar-looking model with a bound f-hole was called the "CO Mark I Model 300."

Celebrity III/Mark I, mid-1960s. $450

Combo/Mark I, mid-1960s. $600

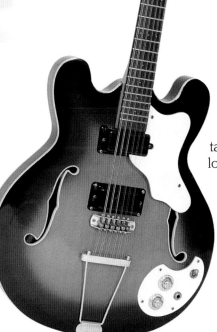

Celebrity III/Mark XII, mid-1960s. $550

The Celebrity series doesn't fetch too much interest (compared to other Mosrites) in the vintage guitar phenomenon. Perhaps it's because they look too much like Gibson 335s and other similar instruments; i.e., other Mosrites have more aesthetic amenities going for 'em. Nevertheless, even Celebritys have thin, lightning-fast necks and unique-sounding Mosrite pickups. The 12-string model shown here is quite easy to play, and get this: Vibratos were optional on Mosrite 12-string models!

Semie Moseley had just opened a Mosrite factory in Booneville, Arkansas (just down the road from the old Gretsch facility) in 1992 when he was diagnosed with multiple myeloma. He passed away on August 7th of that year, and the Arkansas factory closed in 1993. As of this writing, the future of the brand name is uncertain, and has been the subject of rumors and speculation.

CARVIN

One semi-unheralded but historically-important California builder that has been in business for over 50 years is southern California's Carvin company, founded by Lowell Kiesel in 1946. Kiesel began building pickups in his Los Angeles garage, and moved his company to Covina in 1949, then to Escondido in 1967. Carvin occupied more than one facility in that town until 1995, when the company moved into an 80,000 square foot state-of-the-art factory in San Diego.

Carvin, ca. 1965. $350

Carvin's chronology, like many other manufacturers, involved amplifiers prior to guitars. In spite of having been in business for more than a half-century, Carvin hasn't gotten as much recognition as it may deserve, possibly because the company has opted to sell direct to retail customers via catalogs and several retail stores located in southern Cali-   fornia, and, more recently, the Internet. The company *does* have a distribution system to other retail stores in other countries besides the U.S., however (as do other U.S. manufacturers). Carvin (which is still family-owned) must have been doing something right, as they are still manufacturing high-quality instruments and sound reinforcement gear under one roof.

Shown here and on the opposite page are a matching guitar and bass from the mid-60s (the person who owns 'em will only sell them as a set, if and when he opts to sell 'em), as well as an early '80s CM140 Stereo guitar. The latter instrument has some definite Les Paul influences (particularly from the Custom), but it's got an all-maple body and some sophisticated but logical mini-toggle controls. It's a very comfortable guitar that would probably be considered highly underrated by many professional players. The Kahler fine-tune bridge/tailpiece unit was available as an aftermarket accessory, but this one was installed at the Carvin factory.

Carvin bass, ca. 1965.
$350

Carvin CM140 Stereo, early 80s. $400

GUILD

One stereotype that's often heard when classic U.S.-made guitars are being discussed is an opinion that "Guilds are just cheaper copies of Gibsons" (or words to that effect). But how accurate is such a comment? True, some Guilds look quite similar to certain Gibson models, but it's also fair to note that the quality of Guild instruments has been more consistent over the decades than Gibson instruments (in spite of changes in ownership for both companies).

Moreover, the Guild brand is still relatively young. The company was founded in 1952 by Alfred Dronge, a Polish immigrant who had already experienced success in the musical instrument business as both a retailer and an importer of Italian-made accordions. The founding of Guild Guitars, Inc. was directly related to the original Epiphone company, which, as noted in the "Progenitors" chapter, was experiencing its final throes as an independent manufacturer. At one point during its downward spiral, Epiphone signed a manufacturing and distribution agreement with C.G. Conn, Ltd., and Dronge utilized the talents of Epiphone workers who did not want to relocate to Philadelphia, where the Conn company was shifting Epiphone production (such as it was). The manufacturing facilities for the new Guild company were in New York until 1956, when a new factory opened in Hoboken, New Jersey.

Guild's initial production instruments, introduced in 1953, immediately invited comparisons to Gibson and Epiphone guitars, as they were all full-depth, hollowbody electrics. The new manufacturer introduced flat-top acoustics in 1954, and archtop acoustics in 1955, but it would be 1962 before Guild marketed solidbody electric guitars.

The earlier Guild instruments do indeed owe a tip of the hat to their Epiphone ancestors. The 1955 X-350 "Stratford" shown here is quite similar to a top-of-the-line Epiphone Zephyr Emperor Regent, right down to its three pickups and push-button tone control system (but the Epi had a larger body).

X-350 Stratford, 1955.
$1700

Sixties Guild instruments began to look more like their Gibson counterparts, however. This 1961 Starfire II, with its single Florentine cutaway, resembles a Gibson ES-175D or ES-125CD. It's also got *white-faced* DeArmond pickups, which were unique to the Guild brand (check out the same pickups on Gretsch, Standel, and Kustom guitars herein—they're all black-faced models).

Starfire II, 1961. $800

The X-175 Manhattan is another example of Guild's ongoing comparison to Gibson, but this 1975 example has something unique going for it: it's a stereotypical, well-made "jazz box," and features Guild's own humbucking-type pickups, which the company introduced in 1962. However, this X-175 also has a master volume control on the cutaway, near the pickup toggle switch. Reportedly, a master volume control didn't become standard on the X-175 until around 1981 (at which time the pickup toggle switch was moved to the bass-side upper bout), but this extra control appears to be factory-original.

X-175 Manhattan, 1973. $1500

Curiously, some of Guild's "budget" hollowbody electric guitars were among their least derivative. Billed as part of a "Student series," the ST-302 was a thinline electric with double Florentine cutaways (Gibson didn't make a standard production instrument with comparable aesthetics). This first-year model also has the small, single-coil pickups that Guild made for their budget instruments; the in-house nickname for these units was "Mickey Mouse pickups," but one long-time Guild dealer and collector has likened their sound to the "staggered-polepiece" pickups found on some vintage Fender electric guitars. Factor in the "stairstep" pickguard as well as the "Chesterfield" logo that were found on Guild's frontline archtop electric instruments, and you've got a unique-looking, unique-sounding, and easy-to-play guitar that certainly doesn't appear to deserve being pigeonholed with Gibson Melody Makers or Fender Mustangs. A measure of respect might be afforded Guild's "Student series" in today's vintage guitar market, however—this '68 ST-302 would probably fetch more than a '68 Melody Maker or a '68 Mustang (and maybe that's the way things *ought* to be).

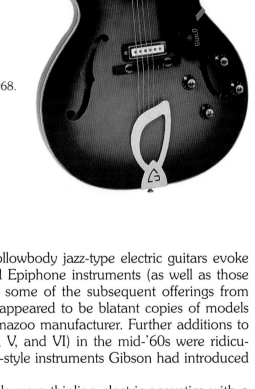

ST-302, 1968.
$850

Starfire IV, 1966.
$1000

Not only did Guild's hollowbody jazz-type electric guitars evoke comparisons to Gibson and Epiphone instruments (as well as those made by smaller builders), some of the subsequent offerings from Dronge's upstart company appeared to be blatant copies of models proffered by the staid Kalamazoo manufacturer. Further additions to the Starfire series (styles IV, V, and VI) in the mid-'60s were ridiculously similar to the ES-335-style instruments Gibson had introduced in 1958.

The new Starfire models were thinline electric-acoustics with a wood block installed in the center of the body, just like their Gibson counterparts. The body style was also remarkably close, so in the case of these models, a "copy" designation doesn't seem to be out of line. The 1966 Starfire IV shown here is a first-configuration model; it would get a master volume control about ten years after its introduction.

In the late '60s, Guild shifted its production facilities to a former furniture factory in Westerly, Rhode Island, and Guild guitars have been continually made at that location to present day.

Guild's solidbody guitar (and bass) experiences made for quite a different chronology, however. As noted earlier (and even though solidbody electrics exploded onto the '50s guitar music scene with a ferocity that was impossible to ignore), Guild didn't begin manufacturing and marketing guitars without holes in them until around 1962.

The first Guild solidbodies looked .... well, different (no Gibson analogies will be cited at this juncture). The body styles looked like some other double-cutaway styles from other companies, except for a crescent-shaped contour that appeared to have been "scooped" out of the end of the guitar body opposite the cutaways. This aesthetic incongruity was actually more functional than it may have appeared; the two extended portions each had a small rubberized tip, which allowed such guitars to be propped up (against an amplifier or some other object) when not in use. In fact, some models of this body style had hinged "kickstands" built into the back of them! The headstocks of Guild's first solidbody instruments still had a "3+3" tuner layout, but their top edge was asymmetrical. The single-pickup Jet-Star/S-50 was the "starter model" of Guild's new solidbody electric guitars, and this 1965 example has all of the unusual facets of the company's initial entries in the solidbody market.

S-50 Jet-Star, 1965. $550

Subsequent solidbody models from Guild looked more, er, "normal" (therefore, more Gibson-like). The Guild S-100, for example, owed a stylistic tip-of-the-hat to the Gibson SG, but the S-100's one-piece neck had a bigger tennon where it joined the body (which would help transfer sound vibrations more efficiently, increasing an instrument's potential for sustain). Most S-100s also had a small pickup phase switch as well. This 1976 S-100 is in a natural mahogany finish, but the model also came in a see-through cherry finish (and those examples *really* looked like SGs). As of this writing, a refined version of the S-100 is the only true American-made solidbody guitar being made by the modern Guild company.

S-100, 1976.
$450

B-302A, 1977.
$450

Guild suffered a major blow when founder Al Dronge was killed in a plane crash in 1972. About five years later, the company went out on a stylistic tangent with their solidbody lineup, introducing a new series of "bell-shaped" instruments that proved to be unpopular (as did some other silhouettes in later years). Nevertheless, the ergonomics and quality of guitars and basses such as this first-year B-302A were quite nice ("A" indicates that the instrument has an ash body and maple neck—standard B-302s had mahogany bodies and necks).

The aforementioned "modern Guild company" was acquired by the Fender musical Instrument Company in 1996. Fender, as noted elsewhere, was never able to market hollowbody electric guitars successfully, and the models currently offered by Guild are based on classic styles from the relatively young brand name (of course, the Fender brand name is only a few years older), and the quality and consistency of the instruments coming out of the Waverly factory is as good as ever.

Gibson's acquisition of the Epiphone company in 1957 ranks among the most memorable (and shrewd) transactions in American guitar-manufacturing lore. Gibson limited their instruments to authorized dealers with protected territories, so the Kalamazoo manufacturer, under the auspices of its forward-thinking and innovative president, Ted McCarty, opted to build Epiphone instruments—*inside the Gibson factory*—that were cosmetically and/or electronically different from Gibson's own guitars and basses. Music stores that were competitors of a Gibson dealer now had an opportunity to retail a brand that was manufactured in the same facilities as Gibson instruments.

It's always interesting to encounter a Gibson-made Epiphone guitar and attempt to ascertain what Gibson model it resembles. In some cases, the differences don't amount to much.

Note that the headstocks of the Sorrento and the Granada have the same silhouette as the '40s Century seen in the "Progenitors" chapter, and the Sorrento even has the same metal nameplate (Gibson used leftover Epi parts on Kalamazoo-made Epiphones until the inventory was depleted).

The Sorrento also has a mini-humbucking pickup, but is pretty much a clone of Gibson's ES-125TC (both models were introduced in 1960). About the only difference in the Granada and an ES-120T is a cream-colored pickguard (and both of those models were introduced in 1962).

Sorrento, 1961.
$750

Granada, 1962.
$650

Gibson-made Epiphone solidbodies generally differed considerably from their Gibson contemporaries. A definitive example is this Wilshire, with a "bat wing" headstock and body silhouette unlike any Gibson. It also has mini-humbucking pickups (not found on standard Gibson solidbodies of the times), and is even a rare "California Coral" custom finish instrument—Epiphone offered Custom Color charts just like Fender and Gibson.

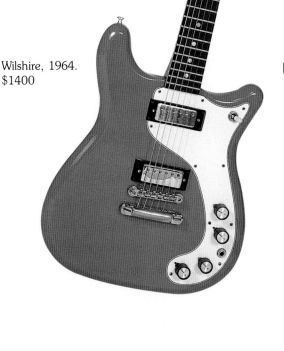

Wilshire, 1964.
$1400

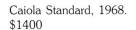

Caiola Standard, 1968.
$1400

Epiphone had endorsement models as well, including two during the Kalamazoo era. Here's a Caiola Standard (in addition to Al Caiola, the other Epiphone endorser was Howard Roberts); while its silhouette is similar to Gibson semi-hollow instruments, its body is fully hollow inside (a la the ES-330) and lacks f-holes. The control layout is definitely pro-oriented, and its headstock shape was a Gibson innovation that appeared on other models as well. It's finished in a non-standard sparkling burgundy color that was also seen on some Gibsons.

Two variants of the Olympic aver that Epiphone student/budget guitars were also marketed. Both examples have a single Melody Maker-type pickup, and the Olympic Special owes a big cosmetic debt to Melody Makers as well. The other Olympic was also available in a two-pickup version.

Gibson's domestic-made Epiphone efforts lasted from 1958 to 1970, at which time the production of the sub-brand was shifted to the Far East, and that's still the case today. However, every once in a while some domestic-made Epis will appear in the musical instrument marketplace (usually as short production runs or limited editions). Gibson still owns the Epiphone name, and can make 'em (or have 'em made) wherever they please.

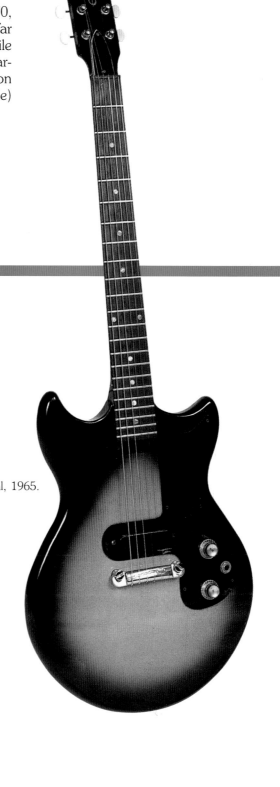

Olympic Special, 1965.
$400

Olympic, 1969.
$350

PEAVEY: THE SOUND OF THE SOUTH

Hartley Peavey doesn't appreciate being compared to Danelectro founder Nat Daniel. Instead, the musical maverick from Meridian, Mississippi has been known to opine that he might deserve a position in the pantheon of musical equipment innovators that's somewhat near the same level (if not in the same echelon) as Leo Fender: "It's interesting that the year Mr. Fender sold his company to CBS, 1965, was also the year I went into business. Sometimes I think that maybe that's the year Mr. Fender 'put his torch down,' and I picked it up."

Heresy? Ego? Hype? Not really, when one considers the time frames in which Leo Fender's company and Hartley Peavey's company introduced their first electric guitars, and the construction methods that were utilized in each scenario. Moreover, Peavey (who acknowledges that Leo Fender was his idol), maintains that like the early (and small) Fender guitar company, the gargantuan manufacturing facilities of the Peavey organization are striving to build and market quality equipment for working musicians at fair prices.

Hartley even thinks that his company's first instrument, the T-60, "...makes a Broadcaster look crude and cheap," and likens a comparison of his T-60 to an old Danelectro product to being kicked in a certain portion of his anatomy. He's got plenty of evidence to support his argument:

When the Peavey T-60 and its companion bass, the T-40, were introduced in 1978, the guitar-manufacturing business sat up and took notice quite quickly. The upstart guitar builder from the Deep South proffered instruments that were manufactured with computer-controlled carving machines; other innovative machinery installed frets and wound pickups, thus assuring consistency in Peavey instruments. The T-60 and T-40 also had several patents, including one for an unusual (and absolutely appropriate) tone circuit, as well as a patent for installing a truss rod into a guitar neck prior to carving, which would "pre-tension" the neck and help it to remain straight.

Most of the earlier Peavey guitars and basses have ash bodies and oiled, natural finishes. Another early aesthetic incongruity was the use of "lightning-bolt P" control knobs (the letter was taken from the company logo). While it would take a while for the company to land major guitar players as endorsers, the T-60 and T-40 were immediately successful among the "general guitar-buying public." Peavey instruments were dependable and durable, and represented an outstanding value to players (full-time and part-time).

So perhaps comparing Peaveys and Danelectros came about because of their respective price points during their respective introductions, and if that's the case, such comparisons aren't valid—in spite of the fact that a T-60 could well have been "everybody's first electric guitar" in the late '70s and early '80s, just as a Silvertone/Danelectro could have been "everybody's first electric guitar" in the early-to-mid-'60s. A T-60, however, is *light years* ahead of a Dano when it comes to quality, and Peaveys epitomize the difference between "value" and "cheap." By the way, the T-60 shown here is N.O.S.!

T-60, 1978.
$350

T-40, 1978.
$250

T-27, ca. 1982. $225

T-25, ca. 1982. $225

T-26, ca. 1982.
$225

Peavey's original "T" series expanded in the early '80s, and the new models came with powerful "Super Ferrite" pickups. About the only differences in the T-25, T-26, and T-27 seen here are the pickup configurations, but note how they have a slightly-more-offset body design than a T-60. The finishes aver that the company was serious about going after its share of the guitar market, and the T-27's standard-for-the-time sunburst finish has somewhat of a "root beer-ish" tinge.

Check out the more shapely contours of the T-20 basses as well, but these models have other intriguing aspects going for them. Note the asymmetrical pickup mounting—according to one source, the larger, curved portion on the bass side of the housing was supposed to function as a thumbrest.

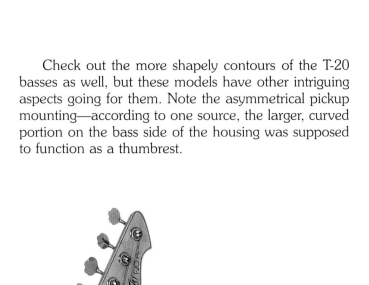

T-20, ca. 1983.
$275

T-20FL, ca. 1982.
$300

However, the natural-finished T-20FL is particularly interesting, as it has a "lined fretless" neck. In lieu of metal frets, this neck simply has lines on a rosewood board, which offers a player the opportunity of plunking a bit more like a traditional upright bass player would. A fretless electric bass is capable of a trombone-like, gliding sound (if desired), and while some cynics have dubbed the markings on necks like this T-20FL's to be "sissy lines," necks on some other fretless electric basses don't have lines—there's just a big piece of wood in front of a player. However, most unmarked fretless necks do have side dot markers—as do fretted and lined fretless basses— for a modicum of reference. While the T-20 was a popular bass among players, as of this writing the T-20FL seen here is the only one this writer has encountered.

The short-scale T-15 and T-30 are utterly unique in American electric guitar lore. They had a Gibson Byrdland-like 23½ inch scale, and their pickup configurations appeared to be a nod to Gibson electrics and Fender Stratocasters (but note where the pickup toggle switch is on the T-15). While budget-priced, T-15s and T-30s were still made in the same facilities as frontline Peavey instruments, and were excellent "starter" instruments for student guitarists. All they did was perform well, and they held up. However, the market apparently didn't want to support a short-scale electric guitar, even in the early '80s "entry-level" market segment. "Great idea ... didn't sell!" states the company's founder.

T-30, ca. 1983.
$150

T-15, ca. 1983.
$150

T-15s and T-30s (as well as some other subsequent early Peavey models) *even came with an amp-in-the-case option* at one point in the early '80s! The amplifier inside the Peavey case was solid-state (which goes without saying), but the Mississippi manufacturer *had* to be expecting yet another Danelectro parallel in minds of many guitar lovers. Such a scenario was practically unavoidable, eh?

The Horizon moniker was seen on more than one early Peavey model, and this one has the first configuration to acquire that name. Its body is a bit more "pointed," but it still has an oiled finish. Like the T-60, this example is N.O.S.

Horizon, early 1980s.
$250

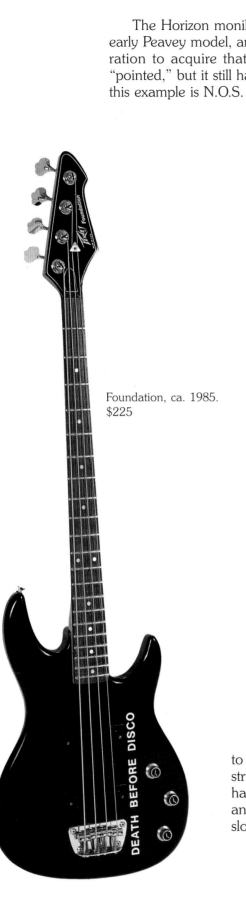

Foundation, ca. 1985.
$225

The longevity of the Foundation bass is a testament to the Peavey company's tenacity regarding quality instruments that play and sound great. This initial version has two Super Ferrite pickups, a simple control set-up, and a slim neck that makes it a delight to play. The, um, slogan is made from "aftermarket" stick-on letters...

Mystic, ca. 1984. $175

Razer, ca. 1984.
$200

Peavey opted to get into the "modernistic-shape" guitar market in 1983, with the introduction of the scorpion-like Mystic and the terrifying Razer. While the Mystic seemed to get its inspiration from brands like B.C. Rich, the Razer looked like...well, like nothing else. In fact, simply *describing* its visuals seems to be a bit of a challenge—"reverse arrowhead with a knee notch" may not sound all that impressive, but that terminology may be the most applicable to the Razer's looks.

However, both the Mystic and the Razer were actually quite comfortable to play. While they'll never attain the respectability as collectible instruments that have been afforded to other "modernistic-looking" guitars from other decades, these two oddball Peaveys might ultimately be able to exploit the ol' "goofy and endearing" syndrome that seems to afflict some guitar enthusiasts. Just give 'em time...

Peavey's subsequent instruments have affected more traditional silhouettes, most likely for competitive reasons as much as anything else, and to some extent that seems to be a bit of a paradox. The Peavey "T" series guitars and basses—as well as other early instruments—were on the cutting edge of guitar-building innovation, and the company is still producing quality guitars, basses, other musical instruments, and sound reinforcement gear that is quite popular and highly-respected by players all over the planet.

Hartley Peavey still isn't satisfied. He's still striving to come up with new and innovative gear for musicians, and he insists: "If it makes sound, it's fair game." Moreover, he's still feisty about the image his products seem to have among guitar snobs: "Of course, every once in a while, someone will tell me something like 'You know, Peavey, you build great stuff,' then they'll add, 'for the money.' Well, bull****. We build good stuff and it holds up. It represents *value*."

Following the initial success of electric guitar innovations in the '50s, companies that were specifically seeking the amplified facet of the guitar market sprang up in California and other locations across the U.S., and over the second half of the 20th Century, builders who thought their ideas would be viable have come and gone. Some companies that specialized in amplifiers opted to try their hand at building and/or marketing guitars, while other totally new operations were the musical equivalent of meteorites, flaming out quite quickly. Let's take a look at some of them (in alphabetical order):

Alamo instruments were made, perhaps not surprisingly, in San Antonio, Texas. The company was a bit of a factor in the budget amplifier field in the '60s, but they also tried their hand at fretted instruments. Many Alamo guitars and basses had unusual bodies that were made of a wood "frame" with tops and backs of thin veneer. That's the case for this mid-'60s Titan, but it also has black-tipped Kluson tuners, which aren't seen too often on Spanish guitars. What appears to be a gouge in the scratchplate is actually a sort of logo that has been referred to as an "Oriental 'A.'" Well, it does look somewhat like an 'A' if viewed vertically (as is the layout here), but guitars are played horizontally. Alamo also made house brands, and a Ryder example, based on a single-pickup Fiesta, shows the unique Alamo bridge/tailpiece, which appears to owe a tip of the hat to Danelectro.

Alamo Titan Mark II, 1965.
$175

Ryder-by-Alamo, ca. 1964.
$150

The New Jersey-based Ampeg amplifier company dabbled in the guitar market on more than one occasion, and their initial efforts concentrated more on basses. Some of the first models were unfretted (to better emulate an upright bass), and were most likely the first instruments of their type to offer such an option (Ampeg's new solidbody instruments debuted in 1966, and Fender's Precision Bass wasn't offered in a fretless version until 1970). This SSUB (Short-Scale Unfretted Bass) is probably one of a kind. It has a full-face pickguard with f-holes routed into it (some full-scale Ampeg basses had f-holes that went *all the way through the body*, but short-scale Ampegs of that time are much rarer).

Ampeg SSUB, 1967.
Probably one-of-a-kind,
$?

Ampeg "See-Through,"
1971. $800

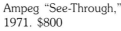

Then there were Ampeg's Plexiglas guitars and basses, which premiered in 1969. They were quite innovative—the guitar had interchangeable pickups to affect different sounds, and the bass was offered in fretted and unfretted versions. The Rolling Stones' Keith Richards can be seen playing an Ampeg "See-Through" in *Gimme Shelter*, a documentary of the band's 1969 tour, and other notable players used Ampeg Plexi models, which are among the most cosmetically-cool electric instruments in history.

Bernie Rico's B.C. Rich instruments offered radical looks *and* radical electronics when they came onto the guitar market in the '70s. They featured exotic woods, exotic shapes, and exotic controls, as epitomized by this 10-string (!) Bich, made in 1978—only the two lowest strings are "singles." The guitar has neck-through construction, and figured maple "wings." It looks like quite a rocketship, and its controls intimate that you'd almost need to be a rocket scientist to play it, for that matter. Like many of the other brands that started out as U.S.-made instruments, B. C. Riches ultimately ended up as overseas-produced instruments, for the most part. Some very-high-end guitars are being produced in the High Desert of southern California on a very limited basis, according to the brand's distributor (for an example, see "Outro/The Beat Goes On"). Rico died in 1999, and his son is attempting to continue his father's efforts.

B.C. Rich Bich, 1978. $1500

Dean ML bass, 1981. $700

Dean Zelinsky founded the company bearing his given name in the late '70s, and his instruments were just as radical-looking as Rico's, although the original Deans seemed to base their shapes on earlier "modernistic" guitars such as the Gibson Explorer and Flying V. Nevertheless, Deans were also noted for their oversized V-shaped headstock, and enthusiastic users included members of Kansas and the Cars. This '81 ML bass is sort of an original shape, but it actually seems to combine the aesthetics of a Flying V (lower bout) *and* an Explorer (upper bout/extended cutaway). Deans also got the "offshore" experience.

An oversized entrant in the "not-necessarily-acoustic" category is this Ernie Ball Earthwood bass. Made from the early '70s to the early '80s, these instruments got their inspiration from a Mexican guitarron. One longtime Ernie Ball employee noted that less than 500 were made, and this example was probably one of the last. The Earthwood series got its name from the use of wood instead of artificial material wherever possible (truss rod cover, fret markers, binding, etc.). This bass is indeed capable of being amplified—there's a transducer built into the bridge, and the cord plugs into the instrument through the strap button on the bottom of the body.

Hallmark/Standel, ca. 1965. $450

Ernie Ball/Earthwood, 1983. $1400

This gold-sparkle instrument is somewhat bizarre, in that it has *two* brands! The headstock bears the Hallmark name—that brand was a short-lived venture for a former Mosrite employee named Joe Hall—but the metal plate that houses the pickups is affixed with a snake-like "S" logo, which is the trademark of the Standel company. This guitar has obvious Mosrite influences, but instruments like this bearing the Standel logo only were advertised in mid-'60s issues of *Downbeat*. For further details, see the Standel brand instruments in this chapter.

The sorta-banana-shaped Hendrick is a mysterious short-lived brand from the early '80s. The instruments were supposedly made in Texas, Ohio, and Michigan. Some Hendricks—not necessarily the last ones made—were reputed to have parts (including necks) from a Japanese guitar company, but were still assembled in the U.S. (the brand's history is *that* nebulous). This example is made of African limba/"korina." It's been estimated that no more than 100 Hendricks were ever made.

Hendrick Generator,
early 1980s. $1500

Maryland's Kapa instruments were made from 1962 to 1970. They were budget-type instruments, made with different parts from different suppliers (the Dutch immigrant who created the line apparently shopped around for the best deals he could get). One of the brand's most popular models was the Continental, a vaguely Fender-ish instrument that appeared in six-string, 12-string, and bass configurations. Some of the 12-string models had vibratos, which would have meant a tuning nightmare for players.

Kapa Continental XII,
mid 1960s. $250

Kapa Cobra, mid 1960s.
$150

Another example of hodge-podge/Frankenstein American electric guitars was Kapa's Cobra model. They may be somewhat rare, but they also came in goodness knows how many styles, as the company would make a run of single-pickup guitars from time to time just to use up extraneous parts. The Cobra wholesaled for $39, and was supposed to be retailed as a leader item for $59. Obviously, such models were never catalogued.

109

The unusual aluminum-neck Kramer line was another brand that made a big splash in the '70s. In addition to the metal neck (with wood inserts), the original Kramer models had Ebonol fretboards (bowling ball material) and a "tuning fork" headstock shape. Critics opined that the neck felt cold, and Kramer ultimately switched to a more traditional solidbody guitar style. Like other brands, the Kramer name has bounced around a lot in the guitar market since its introduction, and as of this writing, is found on an imported series of instruments.

The 450G seen here represents some of the earlier, more-traditional styles of guitar bodies and pickup configurations seen on Kramer instruments (but that tuning fork headstock is still *eye*-catching, ain't it?).

Kramer 450G, ca. 1978. $375

Kramer Stagemaster bass, 1981. $350

Kramer ultimately came up with some original body silhouettes that were slightly different (but weren't particularly inspiring). One wag who saw this early '80s Stagemaster bass commented that a *black*-bodied instrument with such a body would have looked like it belonged to Batman (The "Bat Bass," anyone?). This example has replacement knobs.

110

The headless Duke series was the last of the aluminum-necked Kramers. They owed a cosmetic nod to the Steinberger company, which had originated the headless, downsized look a few years earlier. However, while Steinberger instruments were supposed to use unique, double-ball strings designed and manufactured specifically for that brand's patented tuning system, Kramer Dukes used regular strings—the ball end loaded at the headless end of the neck, and regular guitar tuners were installed on the body. Duke basses only came in a short-scale version, and this one's "Deluxe" designation means that it has an upgrade pickup and bridge, along with a three-way mini-toggle switch that offers different pickup coil sonic options. These instruments are small, lightweight, and a lot of fun to play, which means they ought to appeal to any aging Boomer who still wants to try to gig on weekends, in spite of back and/or hernia problems...

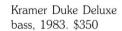

Kramer Duke Deluxe bass, 1983. $350

Kustom K-200A, 1968. $450

Many Boomer enthusiasts probably recall Kustom amplifiers, which were upholstered in tuck-and-roll Naugahyde. A plethora of groovy colors was available, and the company even had a corporate critter, the Nauga—which looked like a cross between the cartoon version of the Tasmanian Devil and a Schmoo from the "Lil' Abner" comic strip—to promote its wares (the mascot was also called the Krazy Kat or Kustom Kat in some ads; it *did* have a vaguely feline or perhaps bat-like appearance). For a brief, shining moment (more like a year and a half), Kustom tried their hand in the guitar market; from approximately mid-1968 to late 1969, some 2000 to 3000 electric guitars and basses were made by Kustom in their Chanute, Kansas facility. All instruments were semi-hollow, and appeared to have Rickenbacker and Gibson SG influences in their body style. They had DeArmond pickups, metal nuts, and slim, fast necks. The top-of-the-line K-200A guitar also had a Bigsby "horseshoe" vibrato.

Among the rarest production instruments in the annals of American guitar folklore are the LaBaye "2 x 4" instruments from 1967. Only 45 were ever made, and they were only shown at one NAMM show; i.e., the line went kablooey on the launch pad. The company was headquartered in Green Bay, Wisconsin, but the instruments were made in Neodesha, Kansas at the Holman-Woodell factory (see the Wurlitzer instruments in this chapter). Apparently designed with minimalism in mind, LaBayes were ahead of their time, perhaps, but even an endorsement by the Robbs (a band that appeared on Dick Clark's "Where The Action Is" television show) didn't help. The instrument shown in ads had regular-looking control knobs (it appears to have been a prototype), but production LaBayes had thumbwheel controls, as seen on this bass. Interestingly, this instrument has a guitar-like scale, which seems to indicate that the company simply slapped different hardware, pickups and other parts on the same bodies they were using for guitars (it appears that the Valco company did the same thing with some of their Res-O-Glas instruments).

LaBaye 2 x 4, 1967.
$600

Magnatone Deluxe
Mark III, 1957. $250

At one time in the chronology of California electric guitar manufacturing, it seemed that the Magnatone company was holding its own with other Golden State builders. They made viable steel guitars and amplifiers, many of which were covered in celluloid ("mother of toilet seat"), and such items were used and respected by notable players (including Buddy Holly, who played through a Magnatone amp). But Magnatone was never a factor in the electric Spanish guitar market—their designs seemed derivative and uninspiring. Note the 1957 Deluxe Mark III shown here—its silhouette is quite similar to Les Pauls of the times, and its only aesthetic incongruities are a full-face Formica-like pickguard and an "M"-cutout tailpiece.

Ditto the '65 Zephyr—it has a center-point vibrato and a sparkle finish, but so what? It looks like yet another Stratocaster copy, for the most part. Nevertheless, instruments from this series were seen in a mid-'90s ZZ TOP video for a song called "She's Just Killing Me," so there's a bit of retro-panache to 'em in some folks' minds.

Magnatone Zephyr, 1965.
$300

Even the venerable Martin company has stumbled on more than one occasion in its attempts to manufacture and market electric guitars. Their first efforts were simple; they merely installed pickups on flat-top acoustic guitars. Once they committed to developing and building electrics, however, the initial offerings were archtop electrics that debuted in the early '60s (and were gone before the decade was over). This GT-75 has a unique double-cutaway design and DeArmond pickups.

Martin's short-lived solidbody effort (1979-'83) appeared to be somewhat halfhearted, as the company used parts from outside sources (DiMarzio pickups, etc.). They're relatively rare, but not particularly desirable, except as utility instruments (at least, that seems to be the case for now...). One wonders to what extent Martin felt like promoting these instruments, as only "CFM" is seen on their headstocks. What's more, the laminated wood stripes in their maple bodies are attractive, but their modified "Viennese" headstocks were just plain homely.

Left: Martin GT-75, 1965, $900. Right: Martin EM-18, ca. 1980. $600

Another Maryland guitar enterprise was the Micro-Frets company, which made instruments from 1967 until around 1974. Unlike Kapa, this brand had some unique construction features, including a tunable nut, bodies that appeared to be solid but were hollow inside (and some of 'em actually snap together!), etc. The Calibra I shown here also has Micro-Frets' patented (for whatever reason) Calibrato vibrato. The extraneous items displayed with it are exemplary of the "Cracker jack syndrome" in the vintage guitar phenomenon; i.e., finding extra "goodies" inside the case of a used guitar makes for an extra "rush" for a lot of enthusiasts. The contents of this guitar's case included a brochure about the tunable nut and Calibrato vibrato, a 1972 retail price list, and an unopened pack of Micro-Frets guitar strings ("with Tri-Metal Tone").

Also seen is a Signature bass from the same time period; it was available in short and long scales.

Micro-Frets Calibra I, ca. 1972. $550 w/ "goodies"

O'Hagan Shark, ca. 1980. $300

Micro-Frets Signature bass, ca. 1972. $300

A fairly recent flash-in-the-pan was the O'Hagan brand, made in Minnesota from 1979 to 1983. No more than 3,000 were made, and one of their positive facets was neck-through construction. While many O'Hagan models bore a resemblance to other classic models from other manufacturers, their first instrument, the Shark, was also their most unusual offering. Its profile was quite distinctive, and part of the hype surrounding this guitar noted that it was comfortable to play *sitting down* (an unusual ploy, but true). O'Hagan used pickups and other parts from outside suppliers, and their instruments may yet attain some degree of respectability in the guitar market as used/vintage instruments than they did when they were new (the Shark would certainly qualify as a "curiosity item").

While the Ovation company certainly turned the acoustic-guitar market on its side in the late '60s with the introduction of its innovative flat-tops (which featured a fiberglass "bowl" instead of traditional acoustic guitar sides and backs), they would experience less success once the company opted to enter the electric guitar field. Ovation's first series was an acoustic-electric line—shades of Martin!—however, the bodies of Ovation's "Storm series" guitars and basses were thinline. Introduced the year after Ovation acoustics premiered, the Storm series was technically discontinued in 1969, but the company used up parts until the early '70s. They actually introduced "new" models in the series after it was discontinued, as exemplified by this model K-1217-5 "Typhoon V" bass, which was first listed in May of 1971, and was discontinued in June of 1972. It has a flat black, textured finish as seen on several latter-day Storm series models.

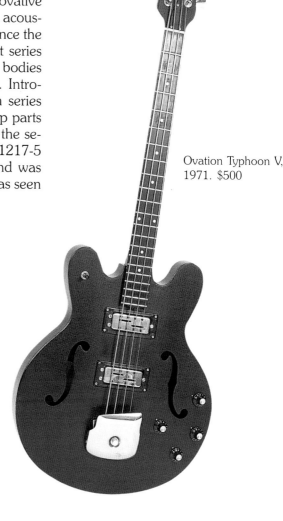

Ovation Typhoon V, 1971. $500

Ovation Breadwinner, ca. 1973. $500

Ovation Deacon XII, 1975. $600

Ovation's first solidbodies premiered in 1971. They weren't particularly successful either, but had some innovative features that give them a bit of distinction in the pantheon of American electric guitars. The first two models, the Breadwinner and the Deacon, were most likely the first *production* instruments with active circuitry. Then there was their improbable "battle axe" profile, which was actually quite comfortable. The basic Breadwinner came in four textured finishes; the "buckskin" color was the third most popular and was the only one with a tortoise-shell pickguard (only blue is rarer). The upgrade Deacon came in a 12-string model, which is a favorite performance guitar of Roy Clark. Ovation tried other, more conventional-shaped instruments in the '70s as well, but they all flopped.

115

Over the decades, some brands names of specific lines of instruments have actually been the monikers of noted players (as opposed to Gibson's "Les Paul model" or Fender's "Eric Clapton Signature Stratocaster"). Veteran "player's player" Roy Buchanan (the subject of an acclaimed PBS special in the early '70s), was best known for his use of a Fender Telecaster, so it shouldn't be surprising that the instruments he helped to design that had his name on their headstocks were Tele-inspired. Built by Fritz Brothers Guitars of Mobile, Alabama in the mid-'80s, Roy Buchanan guitars had active circuitry and a unique pickup switching system that allowed the use of three pickups in any combination. Regrettably, the Roy Buchanan line had only been on the market for about a year when the guitarist died under mysterious circumstances in 1988. Subsequent instruments had "Fritz Bros." on their headstocks, but there aren't many of those around, either.

Roy Buchanan Standard, 1987. $1000

Schon, 1986.
$600

The musical stylings of Neal Schon were just about as different from those of Roy Buchanan as their name brand instruments. Best known for his work with the platinum-selling rock band Journey, Schon was also heavily involved with the creation of the short-lived line that bore his name. In a mid-'90s interview, the guitarist said of his namesake instruments: "I was trying to come up with something that could get several different tones. It actually sounded more like an SG instead of a Les Paul, but you could get 'Stratty' tones out of it as well. I think it ended up with its own, distinctive sound." Schons also featured active circuitry. Some were built in California and others were built in Canada (this one is a U.S.-made instrument). It's questionable how many Schons were ever completed; they're quite rare.

116

To opine that the S. D. Curlee brand was a no-frills line is an understatement. They were built in Matteson, Illinois from the mid-'70s until about 1981, although some legitimate imported Curlees and related brands do exist. These guitars and basses, intended to be inexpensive and practical (right down to the natural oiled finish), had more things going for them than one might think (i.e., don't be put off by the lack of fretboard markers). The construction might be referred to as "nearly-neck-through," as the neck extended all the way to the bridge, but was still a bolt-on. The nut and bridge were made of brass (to affect better sustain), and the earliest brass parts were hand-made. Reportedly the serial number system started at #518, and the bass shown here is #530, so it's not surprising that its bridge looks like a high school metal shop project. Another intriguing feature about the basses were their 32-inch (medium) scale, which was quite unusual for the time.

S.D. Curlee, ca. 1976. $300

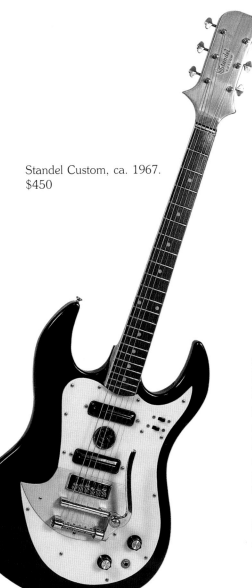

Standel Custom, ca. 1967.
$450

California's Standel amplifier company also attempted to market guitars during its heyday, but the chronology is nebulous—at least three (and perhaps four) builders made Standel brand instruments during the '60s. The earliest and rarest examples were built by Mosrite founder Semie Moseley, then came other Standels made in the Bakersfield area, including the Hallmark/Standel seen earlier, and the solidbody "Custom" seen here. Some guitars and basses with the same neck and headstock as seen on the Custom had fiberglass bodies, a la Valco Res-O-Glas instruments.

This Custom might hold the record for the number of screws installed on a guitar body. It's also N.O.S., having been discovered in the back of a Louisiana music store in 1992.

The final series to bear the Standel logo was quite nice, however, and they were made on the other side of the country. New Jersey's Harptone company created some elegant guitars and basses for the California amplifier company, and such instruments seem to be quite underrated in the vintage guitar market as of this writing. This 1968 510-S thinline has double-Florentine cutaways, extra-wide binding, DeArmond pickups (the same model that Gretsch had stopped using about a decade earlier), and a headstock silhouette not unlike that of an ultra-high-end D'Angelico archtop. Production problems with their solid-state amplifiers forced Standel to close its doors in the early '70s. This guitar has been signed by Standel founder Bob Crooks (1918-1999).

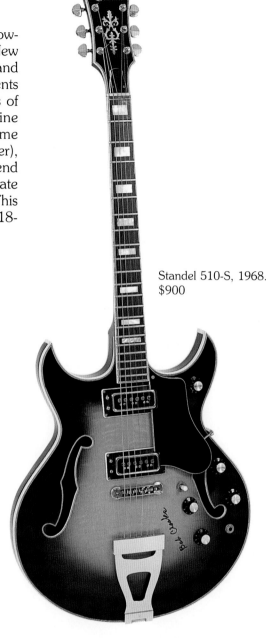

Standel 510-S, 1968.
$900

Travis Bean T-1000
Artist, ca. 1976. $1200

A couple of years before Kramer introduced their aluminum-neck guitars, California motorcycle enthusiast Travis Bean began proffering a similar product. Travis Beans didn't have wood inserts in their necks like Kramers, but they were used by noted players such as Jerry Garcia of the Grateful Dead and the Rolling Stones' Bill Wyman. The instruments were noted for their koa wood bodies, graceful lines, and the "T" logo built into the design of the headstock. Traditional styles such as the T-1000 Artist seen here were the most successful items for the company, but they also made basses and unusual-shaped instruments such as the Wedge series.

118

The T-500 was a lower-priced model that looked more Fender-ish (as opposed to the T-1000's "downsized solidbody version of a Gibson ES-335" vibe). Note the warranty card stuck in the strings—this example was never registered. It, too, is N.O.S., and still has the protective film over the pickguard (look closely at the treble cutaway horn; the material has peeled back slightly in that area). The original Travis Bean company was around for about five years, and the last instruments were made in 1979.

Wurlitzer 2520 Wildcat,
ca. 1966. $300

Travis Bean T-500,
ca. 1978. $800

Keyboard and jukebox giant Wurlitzer also tested the electric guitar markets waters during the '60s "guitar boom". Their instruments were made at the Holman-Goodell plant in Neodesha, Kansas a bit earlier than LaBayes— it appears that Wurlitzers were built from late 1965 through the end of 1966, and possibly into early '67.

Compare the pickups on this 2520 Wildcat (in "Taffy White") and the 2511 Cougar (in "Lollipop Red") to the pickup on the LaBaye bass. The bass' pickup is embossed with the LaBaye brand name, while on these models, the neck pickup is stamped "CHANNEL A" and the bridge pickup is stamped "CHANNEL B"— these were stereo instruments. While there's a normal pickup toggle switch on the bass cutaway, there's also a pickup blend knob on the treble cutaway. The "flying W" cutout in the vibrato is cool, as are the "Rock/Jazz" rocker switches to the left of each pickup, but like most of the brands in this chapter, Wurlitzer's time in the guitar market was somewhat brief.

Wurlitzer 2511 Cougar, ca. 1966.
$300

THE STUDENT SECTION

FENDER

In the autobiography of Fender's Bill Carson (published in 1998), another longtime employee, Charlie Davis, noted: "What a lot of people don't seem to realize is that the bulk of our production was lap steels and student guitars. We'd get a run of Telecasters now and then, and every once in a while some Stratocasters would come through, but we made a lot more Duo-Sonics and Musicmasters back then. I'd say that the production of better guitars didn't pick up until around 1963; maybe that had something to do with the surf music craze."

Regarding student guitars, the same production proportions were also applicable to Gibson. Many more aspiring guitarists started out on Musicmasters or Melody Makers (and *may* have stepped up to Strats or SGs), so in some respects (nostalgia *and* raw production numbers) perhaps this chapter should have been positioned ahead of the "Standards" chapter.

While some may have considered the Les Paul Jr. to have been a type of "starter" guitar, Fender's mid-'50s introductions, the one-pickup Musicmaster and two-pickup Duo-Sonic, were the initial student offerings from either of "the Big Two" guitar manufacturers. Both were ¾-size instruments with a 22½-inch scale, and were finished in a Desert Sand color. Original configurations also had a gold anodized aluminum pickguard. Their silhouettes were similar to that of a Stratocaster, with a parallel "waist" on the body.

Musicmaster, 1958.
$800

Some original-style Musicmasters and Duo-Sonics were seen in other finishes (including an odd Sunburst) as the models' popularity increased, but both guitars underwent a major styling change circa 1964. They received offset bodies (a la the Jazzmaster), and standard finishes were red, white, and a powder blue (other colors would become standard in later years). They also ultimately received an enlarged headstock following the CBS acquisition. The 1966 example shown here is actually a Musicmaster II, which has a Jaguar-like 24-inch scale. The "II" designation was relatively short-lived, as Musicmasters soon became available in either scale, and the 24-inch scale was ultimately the standard length. As might be expected, there was also a 24-inch scale Duo-Sonic II, but both versions of Fender's original two-pickup student guitar were discontinued in the late '60s (Musicmasters lasted until 1980).

Mustang, 1965. $600

Competition Mustang, 1972.
$750

Musicmaster, 1966.
$400

One of the primary factors in the Duo-Sonic's demise was the Mustang, which was practically the same instrument with a newly-developed vibrato system. For a nominal amount more, a budding guitarist could conjure up all kinds of sonic gimmickry with what some cynics dubbed an "idiot stick" (and the term could be applied to any vibrato, not just the Mustang's, if it was being used in a flashy or show-off manner). But any teenager who had a Mustang and a Sears Silvertone "Twin Twelve" amplifier in the mid-'60s was probably better off than many of his/her peers. The standard scale on a Mustang was 24 inches, but 22½-inch scale Mustangs were reported to have been available (anybody ever seen one?).

A "Competition" Mustang, replete with a racing stripe, was offered for about four years. While clean, this burgundy example's originally white racing stripe has affected a pinkish tinge over the decades, as the pigment from the body color has apparently "bled" into the decoration.

Leo Fender was working on a short-scale bass when CBS purchased his organization, so the Mustang Bass ended up as one of the company's first CBS-era introductions. It was a tremendous success, as it was easy and fun to play. The Mustang Bass also came in a "Competition" variant, and was in the Fender line for about a decade and a half.

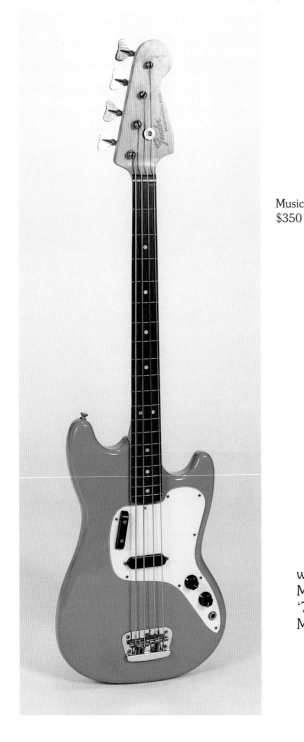

Mustang Bass, 1971.
$650

Musicmaster Bass, 1973.
$350

Interestingly, Fender's second student-grade bass was even plainer than the Mustang Bass. The Musicmaster Bass premiered at the advent of the '70s, and offered fewer frills (but a lower price) than the Mustang Bass.

But what was the big deal about the Bronco? Introduced in 1967, it had one pickup plus a vibrato, and was designed to be sold with a matching amplifier. However, it seemed to be a redundancy, and was another ominous omen regarding CBS-era guitars.

Bronco, 1975.
$325

Melody Maker, 1960.
$600

GIBSON

Gibson's response in attracting fledgling guitarists came along in 1959, with the introduction of the Melody Maker series. The original single-cutaway guitars looked a lot like original Les Paul Juniors, but they had a narrow headstock and small, oval-shaped pickups which resembled the pickups found on Fender's student guitars (and as noted earlier, the same Gibson pickup was found on the ES-120T). The bodies of original Melody Makers were also thinner than other Gibson solidbodies, which undoubtedly evoked "boat paddle" descriptions that were also heard about the Fender Telecaster earlier in the decade. The silhouette and 1 3/8-inch-thick body on this 1960 instrument avers why such a nickname would have been pretty much on the money.

Melody Makers had a total of four profiles during their time. A couple of years after their introduction, the bodies acquired a double-cutaway silhouette, but unlike latter-day Les Paul Specials, Juniors, and SGs, the cutaways on Melody Makers were symmetrical. Another intriguing facet of this 1962 example is its Vibrola, which has the earlier (and lesser-seen) "spoon handle" vibrato arm.

Melody Maker, 1965. $550

Melody Maker D, 1962. $600

The third body style for the Melody Maker closely resembled the second, with a minor difference in the cutaway horns, as well rounder body edges. Cherry finishes became standard, but some sunburst finishes were seen in this configuration as well.

The final incarnation of the Melody Maker series was based, as is obvious, on the SG, Gibson's frontline solidbody in the '60s. Vibrolas *were* standard on this version, and Melody Makers with three pickups, 12-string Melody Makers, and a Melody Maker bass appeared during the production era of the SG-shaped student instruments (which encompassed the latter half of the decade). Regardless of their configuration, all Melody Maker guitars had set-in necks. Many examples have a wide, flat fretboard, and can conjure up an impressive bluesy sound (and these days, such guitars probably conjure up a lot of musical memories as well).

Melody Maker bass, 1968. $800

Melody Maker D, 1968. $550

Here's a pristine example of the aforementioned Melody Maker bass, which is simply an EB-0 with cosmetic differences. Note the slightly different headstock profile (straight sides, silkscreen logo instead of pearl inlay, no "crown" decoration), but the headstock isn't noticeably/proportionally narrower, as was the case on Melody Maker *guitars*. Moreover, this instrument is finished in a "Sparkling Burgundy" color, and it's a bit of a paradox that Melody Maker basses, which were intended for entry-level players, are actually rarer than frontline EB-0 basses of the same era, especially since they're the same instrument!

The other two instruments shown here aren't Fender guitars that happened to be "mis-filed" or re-located due to space problems. They were made in the Gibson factory during the 1960s, and their brand name is that of the city in which they were manufactured. Gibson had placed the "Kalamazoo" moniker on a series of budget instruments in the '30s, and resurrected it for a separate line of electric solidbody guitars and basses. Actually, "solidbody" is somewhat of a relative term when describing '60s Kalamazoos, as their bodies were made of molded chipboard/particleboard/composition board...i.e., sawdust and glue.

It's not out of line to surmise that in the battle between Gibson and Fender for their respective shares of the student market, the veterans in Michigan "blinked" first, because the 1966 Kalamazoo KG-l sho' looks like it could've been made in Fullerton, California. Note the offset, Jazzmaster-like body, the six-on-a-side headstock with a vaguely Fender-ish silhouette, and the bolt-on neck. This KG-1 is the series' "starter" model, with one Melody Maker-type pickup.

Kalamazoo KG-2A, 1969. $250

Kalmazoo KG-1, 1966. $175

Around 1968, the Kalamazoo line assumed a body style similar to the SG (as well as Melody Makers of that time), but those bodies were also made of particleboard, and the instruments still had a bolt-on neck. This 1969 KG-2A was the top of the line guitar (such as it was) of the Kalamazoo brand, with two pickups and a vibrato.

Most likely, the distribution scenario regarding instruments made by Gibson was "three-tier"—Gibson, Epiphone and Kalamazoo. Big changes were in the wind at the advent of the '70s, of course, as the original Melody Maker series as well as the Kalamazoo line were discontinued.

SORDID SEVENTIES SAMPLES & EARLY EIGHTIES ODDITIES

One of the primary reasons this tome sought to use the mid-'80s as a demarcation line/end point regarding instruments that fit its format concerns changes in ownership for Fender (1985) and Gibson (1986). While the purchasers of each company differed considerably (Fender's new proprietor was a group of Fender employees and outside investors who were also in the music business; Gibson was acquired by a trio of Harvard MBA graduates), both manufacturers experienced noticeable turnarounds in their sales and the quality of their instruments as the policies of the new owners were instituted. It took years, but both Fender and Gibson are once again in the driver's seat(s) regarding the position of pre-eminence in the electric guitar industry.

However, things really started to head down the proverbial "toidy" for Fender and Gibson about a decade and a half before each company was sold. It seemed like CBS (owners of Fender from 1965 to 1985) and Norlin (Gibson proprietors from 1969 to 1986) could have cared less that the new models they were introducing were deemed as inferior by many working musicians, and the same was said regarding some "refined" versions of original Fender and Gibson classic models. Quality control was abysmal as well. The redoubtable Gretsch brand was also having its share of problems around the same time, as we'll soon see.

One of Fender's biggest debacles in the '70s was the installation of a new three-bolt, "tilt-neck" system, utilizing a "bullet" truss rod (so named because the adjustment juncture had a bullet-shaped protrusion) on some of the company's classic models. Players complained that the new system wasn't stable, from both a structural and sonic aspect (as for the latter problem, "...you couldn't tell the difference without an oscilloscope," noted Bill Carson). Curiously, the original standard Fender guitar and bass, the Telecaster and the Precision, maintained an original four-bolt neck attachment profile during this time, while the new three-bolt/"bullet" truss rod system was adapted to standard Stratocasters and Jazz Basses.

The 1979 "hardtail" (no vibrato) Stratocaster seen here actually has a bit of "double jeopardy" going for it. Not only does it have the three-bolt/"bullet" truss rod neck attachment system, it's also finished in the weird, ghost-like "Antigua" finish, which was available on all frontline and student Fender instruments in the late '70s. The finish *and* moniker had been assigned to an entire series of Coronado instruments almost a decade earlier, and why the company opted to resurrect this unusual color scheme is anybody's guess. To some cynics, the Antigua finish looks like the yolk of a hard-boiled egg.

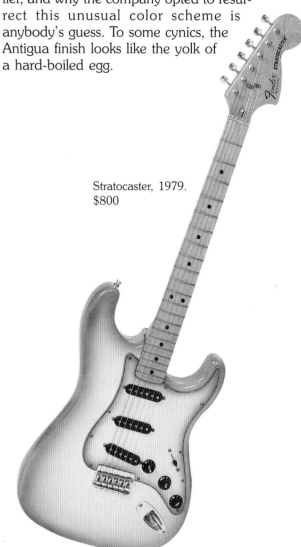

Stratocaster, 1979.
$800

Standard Telecasters may have stayed with the "four-bolt" configuration, but some new Telecaster models did acquire the new neck-mounting system, as well as derivative features that warped the Telecaster model name (and sonic reputation). This Telecaster Custom is exemplary (and it differed, of course, from the double-bound Custom Telecaster that debuted in 1959). Note the Gibson-like control layout as well as the humbucking pickup with offset "3 + 3" polepieces.

Telecaster Custom, 1973.
$850

Jazz, 1978.
$900

The '78 Jazz Bass seen here has a mixture of desirable and "diss-able" features. Its original finish is a translucent reddish-brown (not the standard walnut as seen on other Fenders of that era) that is quite unusual, therefore hard to identify. But this bass also has hard-to-see pearl block inlay on a maple fretboard, as well as three-bolt/"bullet" truss rod construction—dumb and dumber...

The sunburst '83 Strat on display is probably the worst incarnation of the venerable instrument in its entire history. By the early '80s, Fender had reverted to a four-bolt neck system across the board, but this version had a dangerous right-angle jack, two knobs, and a vibrato system that not only operated in one direction (it could make the guitar go flat, but not sharp). The vibrato springs were mounted *under the pickguard*, in a cavity on the *top* of the body, necessitating removal of the pickguard to adjust spring tension. This variant of the Strat was indeed loathsome, and mercifully, it was only around for a couple of years.

Stratocaster, 1983.
$600

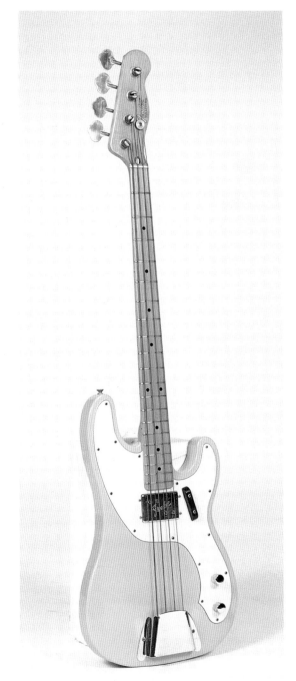

Telecaster Bass,
1973. $750

Fender introduced the Telecaster Bass in 1968, and the original version was a clone of the plank-bodied, early '50s Precision Bass. However, the model switched to a three-bolt/"bullet" truss rod construction configuration in the early '70s, and also acquired a Fender humbucking pickup with offset "2 + 2" polepieces that was positioned closer to the neck. As a result, this second variant was not only cumbersome, it had a muddled sound as well. Fender's humbucking pickups (on guitars *and* basses) didn't offer any distinctive tones; accordingly, this bass didn't "moan and groan;" it just kinda "grunted".

The new models introduced by CBS/Fender didn't fare any better than revised versions of long-standard guitars and basses. In some respects, the cards were stacked against them right out of the chute, but their lack of success during their time, coupled with the proportionate lack of interest in them these days as either collectibles or classic-sounding instruments, seems to confirm their stereotypical low status in the fretted instrument marketplace, then and now.

And the bizarre Starcaster probably epitomizes the oddball instruments and wrong turns inextricably intertwined with Fender's CBS era better than any other guitar. Introduced in 1976 and outta there by the end of the decade, it was another attempt by the solidbody-oriented company to develop and market a thinline hollowbody-type electric guitar. One would think Fender should have learned a lesson with the Coronado series, and from an aesthetic standpoint, the Starcaster looked even more oddball and "un-Fenderish" than the previous hollowbody series. Perhaps it's not surprising the Coronados included several models of guitars and basses, but Starcaster production consisted of one homely instrument. An obvious starting point is its body; yes, the offset style is indeed quite comfortable, but let's tell it like it is: This guitar looks lopsided. There is, however, an important construction difference in the Starcaster and the Coronado series—the Starcaster body has an internal solid wood block, a la Gibson's ES-335 (a 1976 Fender catalog describes the Starcaster as "the all-new semi-acoustic electric guitar," and notes that "a solid center block of seasoned hardwood minimizes feedback and provides maximum sustain"). Electronically, the Starcaster has two Fender humbucking pickups, and an extra Master Volume control knob (why?). The chrome-skirted knobs themselves have an almost "industrial" look, and appear to have been better-suited for placement on amplifiers. That was exactly the case for the Starcaster's knobs—they first appeared on a short-lived group of solid-state amplifiers called the Zodiac series, circa 1969-71 (CBS/Fender solid-state amplifiers of the late '60s and early '70s were another huge debacle for the company). The neck is the three-bolt/"bullet" truss rod configuration, of course, and a maple fretboard on a thinline electric guitar looks out-of-place and just plain weird to a lot of observers. Note the headstock silhouette, and compare it to the one on the Micro-Frets guitar seen in the "One-Shots" chapter. Micro-Frets went out of production around 1972, so this headstock profile could lend itself to speculation about the inspiration for its design. If a player owns a Starcaster and enjoys its sound and feel, more power to him/her, but this short-lived instrument was an amalgamation of almost all of the awkward and/or absurd ideas incorporated by CBS/Fender during its two-decades-long legacy of manufacturing and marketing mis-steps...whew!

Starcaster, 1977.
$1300

130

The Lead series lasted longer (1979-82) than perhaps it should have. Apparently, it was supposed to be some sort of a "budget Strat" type of lineup, but no famous player was closely associated with 'em. Lead models simply didn't offer anything spectacularly different from other Fender models, and Fender's 1982 decision to import authorized/legitimate instruments—most of which were classic Fender styles such as Stratocasters and P-Basses—was also probably a factor in the termination of the Lead series.

Lead II, 1980. $300

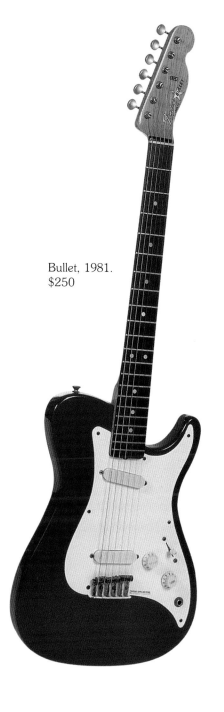

Bullet, 1981.
$250

Fender's last domestic fling at a budget series of guitars was 1981's Bullet series. They were offered in several different models for a short time before production was shifted overseas. Perhaps the most unusual variant was the original model, which had a textured *metal* pickguard, one section of which flipped up at a right angle to accommodate the individual bridge saddle screws. The strings anchored into this part of the pickguard as well, making it an unusual-but-functional innovation. One vintage guitar dealer was displaying a short-lived U.S.-made Bullet at a guitar show a while back with a sign on it, proclaiming that the guitar "never made the boat ride"...

It's intriguing that the other half of "the Big Two" also opted to manufacture and market its own unique and oft-maligned instruments during the '70s and early '80s as well. Like Fender, Gibson's ownership had changed, and quality seemed to get subordinated to quantity. Moreover, like its California competitor, the Kalamazoo company introduced revised versions of standard models (or slightly different replacements) as well as completely new series of instruments that were stunningly unsuccessful in their time, and that still don't fetch much interest among collectors and enthusiasts (although many of them are quite viable as utilitarian instruments, of course). Since Gibson was a more diverse company than Fender regarding its models, it should almost go without saying that they had more models that fit into the category of this chapter.

As noted earlier, Gibson began re-introducing single-cutaway Les Paul models in the late '60s, and even those classic models weren't exempt from an occasional bizarre cosmetic variant. This circa 1974 Les Paul Custom has all of the usual appointments for the model, except for the obvious (and hard-to-rationalize) maple fretboard with hard-to-see pearl block markers, so Fender didn't have an exclusive with "visually-challenging" fingerboards in those times.

The Paul, 1978.
$500

Les Paul Custom, ca. 1974. $1400

At the other end of Gibson's single-cutaway spectrum, a no-frills guitar called simply The Paul was an apparent attempt to garner a share of the budget guitar market. This instrument has a 1978 serial number (the model wasn't reportedly shipped until 1979, but had been announced by the company the previous year). Its, uh, features (or lack thereof) included a walnut body and open-coil humbucking pickups—sometimes guitarists will remove covers from humbuckers in an effort to improve a guitar's sound (and there's been an ongoing debate about whether or not that modification works), but this one didn't have any to start with. Note the unusual location of the toggle switch and lack of a pickguard as well. Gibson introduced other plain-looking, lower-priced guitars over the next few years, but they weren't highly-regarded, and seemed to be a contradiction to the venerable, if rapidly tarnishing at the time, Gibson "image."

V-II, 1980. $750

Gibson even tried radical approaches with its already-considered-radical body styles in this dismal era. The V-II of the late '70s and early '80s was one of the most bizarre instruments the company ever marketed, and while it was a failure as a new instrument, may ultimately attain a bit of collectibility in the vintage market (but don't take that to the bank). The V-II isn't particularly rare, but it's got a few things unique to its style, including a laminated and sculptured body made of walnut and maple, as well as heart- or boomerang-shaped pickups that were only found on this model (in looking back at the V-II's history, a Gibson vice-president noted that the pickups were designed to have "a silvery, Strat-like sound"). It also had nominal upgrade features like gold hardware and an ebony fretboard, and is just weird enough overall to merit some attention from some collectors because of its one-of-a-kind features, so it may be an exception to some of the voluminous stereotyping concerning instruments made during its time.

The V, 1984. $600

Another now-vanquished V-shaped variant went in an opposite direction concerning the aesthetics of its body. The short-lived The V may have had an arrow-shaped silhouette, but its non-traditional guitar shape sported a very traditional Gibson look concerning its construction and cosmetics. A figured maple cap was on top, and The V also had traditional Gibson finishes—cherry sunburst on this example (as seen on Les Pauls and other guitars). The pickups on this model were open-coil type. Note the tuning keys on this instrument, which have flip-out levers to facilitate quicker string winding.

133

One stereotype of the ES-325TD is that it was a replacement for the ES-33OTD, but unlike the earlier model, which (as noted previously) was fully-hollow inside, the ES-325TD had a center wood block like the majority of Gibson models with this silhouette. Nevertheless, the ES-325's other differences weren't particularly inspiring. It had mini-humbucking pickups and just one f-hole. The controls were mounted in an easy-to-install semi-circular plastic plate, and its finishes were usually the drab walnut and cherry colors seen on many early '70s Gibson instruments. Introduced in 1972, this model was gone about six years later.

ES-325, ca. 1974.
$700

L-6S Deluxe, 1975.
$500

Gibson's *new* solid body models during the '70s and the first half of the '80s seem to have been every bit as off-the-beaten-path for the company as Fender's instruments of the same era were for the California company. Gibson had already stumbled in the late '50s, in some respects, with these modernistic instruments, but these new models also flew in the face of the "traditional" perception of the Kalamazoo manufacturer in the guitar-making field. If Gibson was trying to "shake up" the marketplace, its strategy nearly brought the company to bankruptcy. Moreover, the cost-saving measures instituted in the manufacturing process resulted in cheap-looking instruments and shoddy workmanship.

Some of the new introductions seemed to have some commendable ideas, however. The L-6S may have had a profile that made it look like a Les Paul that had been run over by a steamroller, but it was also the first Gibson guitar with a 24-fret neck (two octaves) and powerful Super Humbucking pickups. The original L-6S was introduced in 1973, and had a confusing six-position rotary switch plus a mid-range control in addition volume and tone knobs; it was re-named the L-6S Custom when a less-fancy (therefore less-complicated) version called the L-6S Deluxe was introduced in 1975. Neither model is particularly rare or desirable, but to some players, an L-6S is a great utilitarian guitar. The L-6S Custom was discontinued in 1980, and the Deluxe was terminated the next year.

If Gibson "blinked" concerning bolt-on necks in the budget/student segment of the guitar market in the mid-'60s (on the Kalamazoo sub-brand), they continued the tradition the next decade by applying the same construction features to new *frontline* instruments. Debuting in 1975, the Marauder had a Flying V-type headstock, a humbucking pickup in the neck position, and a large single-coil pickup in the bridge position. Note that the pickups are "see-through" (they're set in clear epoxy). Some variants of this model had a rotary/pan switch to blend the output of the pickups (instead of the usual three-position toggle switch), which wasn't as practical as it might have initially seemed to some players.

Marauder, 1975. $400

S-1, 1976. $400

The S-1 had circuitry designed by pickup innovator Bill Lawrence, who is reported to have described the model as having one pickup with three coils instead of three pickups. Similar to the Marauder regarding its profile and construction, this 1976 S-1 has the short-lived rosewood fretboard that originally appeared on the model (more about fretboards on new models in the '70s a bit later).

135

If Firebirds looked like melted Explorers, then maybe it's fair to say that RDs looked like melted Firebirds, but RDs were in an underclass by themselves. At least they had set-in necks, but they looked and felt awkward. Many (if not most) RDs had "Artist" active circuitry built into them (designed by the Moog synthesizer folks), which was quite confusing regarding its use. Artist circuitry was subsequently installed on other instruments such as Les Pauls; perhaps it was simply an effort to deplete inventory. The RD Standard was around for about two years, and featured a control layout like most other frontline Gibson solidbodies with glued-in necks. It had a Fender-like 25½-inch scale, whereas some other RD models had a normal Gibson 24¾-inch scale. Ergonomically, the RD body felt okay when it was being played in a seated position, but it seemed to protrude too much to a player's left if played in a standing position. Veteran guitarist/song writer Jim Peterik of the Ides of March and Survivor (he sang lead vocals on the 1970 smash hit "Vehicle") is one collector who's enthusiastic about the possible increase of interest in Gibson's sculpted V-II (cited earlier) as a collectible instrument, but he doesn't think much of the RD series, even though RDs and V-IIs were in Gibson's lineup around the same time. Peterik describes RDs as "butt-ugly," and has the time-in-grade to know what he's talking about.

RD Standard, 1977.
$500

SB-450, early '70s.
$450

A series of guitars and basses introduced in the early '70s were apparently supposed to supplant the Melody Maker line, but they had "chunkier" SG-style bodies and lousy, uninspiring finishes (as did some frontline SGs, for that matter!). Models came and went with startling frequency in the budget segment of Gibson's offerings back then. The SB-450 was the top-of-the-line bass (such as it was) in this particular niche, with two pickups and a full-scale neck. Note the controls in the half-moon-shaped, top-mounted plate.

Another low point for Gibson during this oft-maligned era had to have been the Sonex series of guitars. The bodies of these instruments were made of a composite, which meant that their construction wasn't too far removed from the Kalamazoo instruments of the '60s (the "Multi-Phonic" bodies of Sonex guitars consisted of a wood core and a resin exterior). The neck was a bolt-on type, and the headstock sported a new, non-script type logo. This example appears to have a replacement pickup, but there's a tendency to say "who cares?"—this series *was and is* that uninspiring.

Sonex-180 Deluxe, 1982. $225

XPL, 1985. $550

And the same line of thinking just about applies to the '85 XPL Custom seen here—what it was supposed to accomplish in the retail market is anyone's guess. Its angular body style isn't anything innovative ("ya seen one pointy headstock git-tar, ya seen 'em all"), and even though this example is a "Custom Shop Edition" (no more than 200 made), it simply doesn't excite most knowledgeable guitar enthusiasts. Perhaps it seems fitting that this XPL was made in the last year of Gibson's ownership by the Norlin conglomerate (one can almost hear a Bronx cheer in the background...).

As noted earlier, Gibson's bass models also didn't have much success in the '70s and early '80s. In all honesty, the basses offered by the company following its 1986 sale haven't been particularly popular, either—Gibson has never really been a serious factor in the electric bass market, in spite of the relative popularity of their '60s short-scale models.

The electric basses marketed by the Kalamazoo company in the '70s simply add a nominal amount of validity to the preceding pronouncement. Exemplary models included a trio of basses that had the same body silhouette and a 34½-inch scale: the Ripper, Grabber, and G-3.

The Ripper was the first and fanciest of this dubious triad. Introduced in 1973 as the L9-S, it acquired its more hotshot (and marketable?) moniker the next year. The model reportedly started out with a maple body and a bolt-on neck (this writer has never seen a Ripper with a bolt-on neck); its configuration switched to an alder body and set-in neck in 1975. Rippers had a four-position rotary switch, somewhat like an EB-3, and a semi-complicated three-knob control system, somewhat like an L-6S Custom; they were also the only model of this trio to feature a traditional-shaped Gibson headstock. Among the noted players who used Rippers in the '70s were Mel Schacher (Grand Funk Railroad), Greg Lake (Emerson, Lake & Palmer), Rick Danko (the Band) and session ace Carol Kaye...but none of these bassists stuck with the model for an extended period of time.

Ripper, ca. 1974.
$550

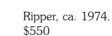

Grabber, 1979.
$375

The single-pickup Grabber was decidedly different, sporting a bolt-on neck during its entire production run, and its pickup was movable—sliding it towards the neck evoked a deeper tone; sliding it towards the bridge evoked a brighter sound. Note the Flying V-style headstock as well. About the only notable appearance of this model was in the hands of KISS's Gene Simmons on the cover of that band's first live album.

The general perception of the three-pickup G-3 is that it was the bass equivalent of the S-1 guitar model, but the G-3 was introduced first. Like the Grabber and the S-1, it had a bolt-on neck and a semi-pointed headstock.

Note the fretboards on all three basses—they're maple, with pearl dot inlays as found on some new Gibson guitars from that decade. The 1978 Fender Jazz Bass seen earlier in this chapter has pearl *blocks* on a maple fretboard, so it appears that "the Big Two" had similar lines of thinking concerning hard-to-see position markers. '70s Gibson basses got a minor amount of notice—primarily from players—when Krist Novoselic, bassist for platinum-selling grunge band Nirvana, was seen whomping such instruments onstage in the early '90s.

G-3, 1980.
$375

Victory MV-II, 1981. $400

Victory, MV-X, 1981.
$400

The last gasp by Norlin/Gibson in marketing an *entire series* of new instruments was the Victory lineup of guitars and basses, which was made from 1981 to 1984. This aggregation seemed to have derived its inspiration from more than one source—the headstock silhouette was reminiscent of a Firebird or Thunderbird (and the Victory series owner's manual noted such), while the severely-offset cutaways seemed to be a nod to the angular instruments associated with "heavy metal"/"hard rock" music around that time (but at least it ain't as "pointy" as the aforeseen XPL). The offset fretboard markers are a nice and practical touch, but similar types of inlay had been seen previously (Gretsch's "thumbprint" markers, for example).

The aforementioned severely-offset body style is quite comfortable—the neck's position almost makes a player think he/she is handling a three-quarter scale instrument. The MV-II ("MV" = "Multi-Voice") was the more basic of the guitars; the owner's manual states that it "... is designed primarily for the discerning country player." It had two open-coil humbucking pickups and a coil-tap switch to affect a single-coil sound. The MV-X was even more complex than it looks, as the middle pickup is not a single-coil type; it's a "stacked" humbucker, with its coils lined up one on top of the other (instead of the usual side-by-side configuration).

Victory basses apparently wanted to be Fender basses *real* bad. They had bolt-on necks, and their large maple bodies made them excruciatingly heavy. A two-pickup bass with active circuitry, the Victory Artist, was also manufactured, but the two-pickup passive Victory Custom seen here is much rarer (only 250 made).

Victory Standard bass, 1981. $400

Victory Custom bass, 1982. $450

Fender and Gibson didn't have a monopoly on the '70s as a decade for manufacturing and marketing oddball instruments that were unsuccessful, and that are not held in high esteem by guitar buffs these days. The Gretsch company was purchased by Baldwin Piano and Organ Company in 1967, and the keyboard-oriented conglomerate moved guitar production to Booneville, Arkansas in 1970. The paradox of re-locating a long-time New York instrument manufacturer to a small town in the Ozark foothills is intriguing, to say the least. While many of the guitars and basses made during the "Baldwin era" of Grestch's history are fine instruments (the 1980 Country Club in the Gretsch chapter, for instance), the Booneville operation also had its share of problems, and a number of unusual Gretsch items that seemed to be "contradictory" to the brand's name and status in the guitar market were made during the decade that the Arkansas factory was in operation.

Some of the most often-maligned Baldwin-era Gretsches were solidbodies, and Arkansas instruments were often fitted with imported pickups. The Committee seemed to be a commendable effort; it had a laminated, neck-through construction style, and was made from walnut and maple. Note the smoked/tinted pickguard, and the fretboard inlay—why did Gretsch see fit to change the inlay pattern starting on the ninth fret, of all places?

TK-300, 1977.
$300

Committee, 1978. $450

The TK-300 probably represents the absolute nadir of instruments that ever bore the Gretsch name. It's comfortable, but it has a bolt-on neck, and its aesthetics are abominable to most Gretsch purists. Check out the angular, asymmetrical body profile, as well as the oversized hockey-stick headstock. It actually resembles the blade of its namesake more than headstocks on Fender 12-string instruments, which have had the same term applied to them by vintage guitar aficionados. Committee and TK-300 series Gretsches were also available in bass versions.

The BST/"Beast" aggregation was the final solidbody series of Gretsch's "Baldwin era," and it showed. Such instruments were varied in their construction, but didn't amount to much concerning their looks, sound, or success in the market. This model 1000 BST has a mahogany body, a bolt-on neck, and open-coil humbuckers. The body silhouette is somewhat interesting for a single-cutaway guitar, and could be found on other Arkansas-made Gretsches as well.

BST 1000, 1979.
$325

Atkins Super Axe, 1978.
$1000

A similar silhouette was found on the Atkins Super Axe, the most innovative idea to emerge from the Ozarks in the '70s. A wide and thin solidbody that was Chet Atkins' final project with the Gretsch brand before he switched his endorsement to Gibson, the Super Axe looked a mite unusual, but featured active electronics (compressor and phaser) which could evoke numerous sounds.

The Gretsch family ultimately re-acquired the rights their namesake brand, and Gretsch instruments are now assembled in Japan, using American and Japanese components. Their quality is among the highest ever for Gretsch guitars and basses, which seems to be yet another (but not surprising) paradox.

142

Les Paul Custom,
1961. $4000

At various times during the respective chronologies of Fender and Gibson electric guitars, each company has marketed certain instruments that were sort of "in between" major changes in the manufacturers' product lines. Other "transitional" guitars from "the Big Two" have simply been items designed to use up leftover parts from other series of instruments. A cosmetic change here and there, and a brand-new model was suddenly being proffered (and it's interesting to speculate about how much advertising and/or hype by company reps was needed to get rid of such "step-children").

As the more diverse company, Gibson had more opportunities to stumble with certain facets of its product line, but among the most desirable transitional instruments in the vintage guitar phenomenon are the SG/Les Pauls of the early '60s. Such guitars were called "Les Pauls" when they were introduced, because the endorsement agreement between company and artist was still valid, but it didn't last long after the re-styled guitars hit the market (and there are various legends and recollections about why Les Paul withdrew his name association with Gibson at that time).

The new instruments had a much more radical look than their original single-cutaway Les Paul forebearers. The bodies of the new instruments were thinner, and the nearly-symmetrical double-cutaway silhouette allowed access to all frets. The sharp profile of the cutaway horns was quite a departure for the staid Gibson company as well. As noted earlier, the series maintained the same general pickup and inlay features as their respective single-cutaway predecessors, as exemplified by the SG/Les Paul seen here.

This Les Paul Custom has a standard white finish, three pickups, and gold hardware (including a "spoon handle" Vibrola), and its decorative ebony and pearl tailblock is original, but rare.

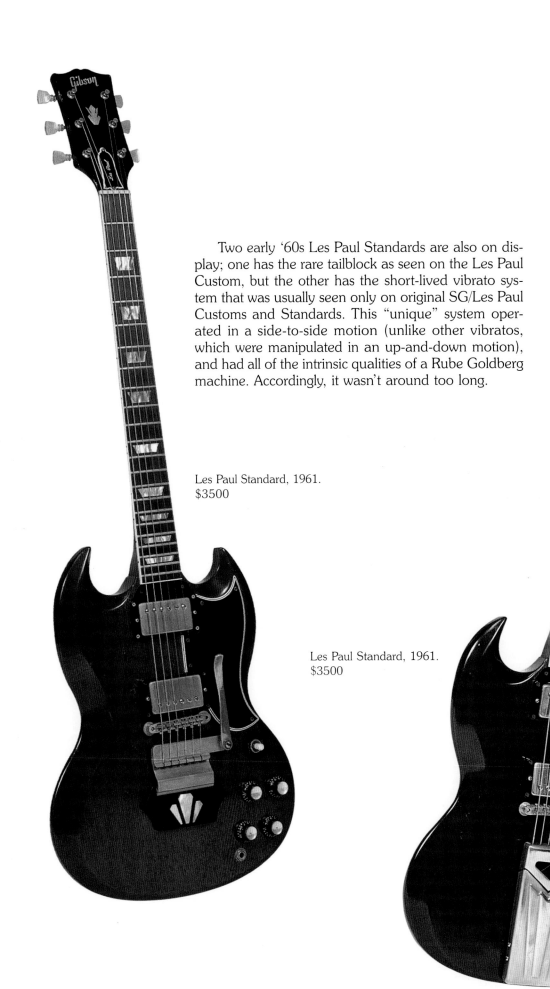

Two early '60s Les Paul Standards are also on display; one has the rare tailblock as seen on the Les Paul Custom, but the other has the short-lived vibrato system that was usually seen only on original SG/Les Paul Customs and Standards. This "unique" system operated in a side-to-side motion (unlike other vibratos, which were manipulated in an up-and-down motion), and had all of the intrinsic qualities of a Rube Goldberg machine. Accordingly, it wasn't around too long.

Les Paul Standard, 1961.
$3500

Les Paul Standard, 1961.
$3500

There have been other times when Gibson's so-called rare birds were, for all intents and purposes, "floor-sweep" models. This 1982 Firebird II is extremely rare; a former Gibson historian speculates that around 100 were made. However, all it amounts to is an attempt to use up parts from the much-maligned RD Series guitars and Artist active circuitry. Technically, it's the only so-called "Firebird" with a bound, flame maple top, full-size humbucking pickups, a non-sculpted "reverse" headstock with "regular" tuners (although a few transitional '60s Firebirds with features from "reverse" and "non-reverse" series had such), and of course, it's the only Firebird with active circuitry, but is it a so-called "collector's item?"

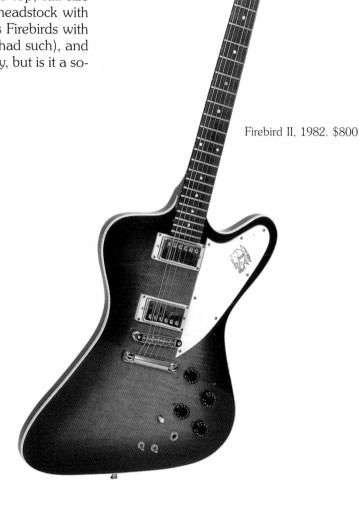

Firebird II, 1982. $800

Swinger/Musiclander, 1969. $1100

Fender wasn't immune from mis-cues either, particularly during its CBS years. One attempt at using up left-over bodies in 1969 wasn't even catalogued, and this chopped-up oddity went by more than one moniker—it's been called the "Swinger," "Musiclander," and "the arrow guitar." Note that the headstock only has the Fender logo (although "Swinger" was seen on some). It appears to be simply a modified Musicmaster, but one source noted that every example he perused had the body of a Bass V, a short-lived '60s five-string bass.

This 1972 Telecaster Thinline is a "legitimate" transitional Fender. When the Fender Company instituted its big manufacturing changes in the early '70s the new Tele Thinline got two new Fender humbucking pickups, and mahogany bodies were discontinued. However, some examples of second-generation Thinlines with mahogany bodies do exist, and that's exactly what this one is.

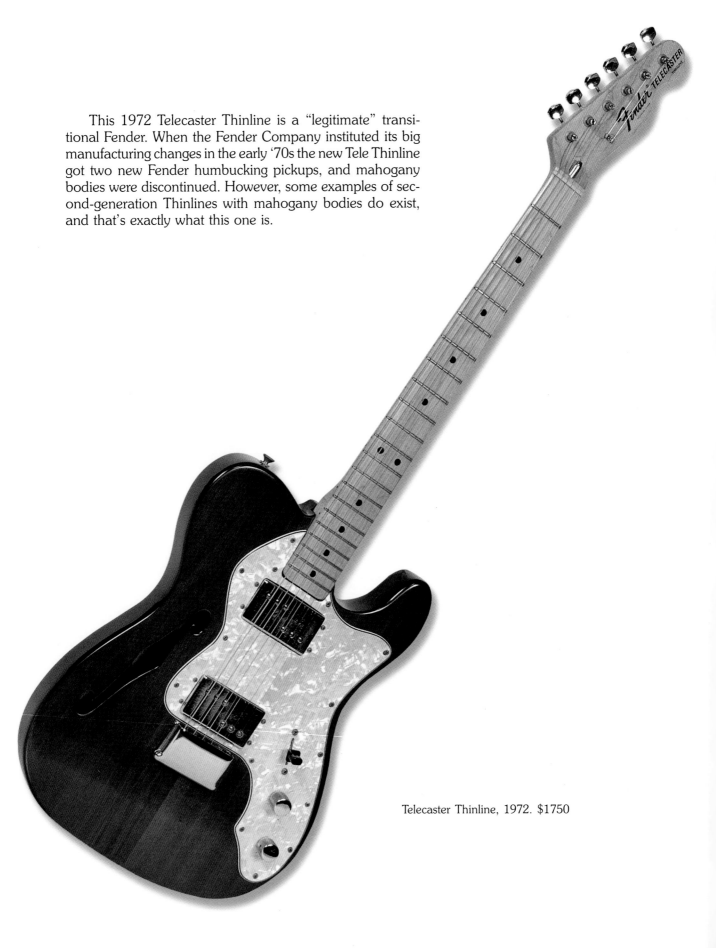

Telecaster Thinline, 1972. $1750

THE FURTHER ADVENTURES OF LEO FENDER

Sting Ray bass, 1978.
$1800

Sabre I, 1978.
$400

One of the most unusual scenarios in the history of the vintage guitar phenomenon occurred in March of 1991, during the load-in for a major guitar show. Word began circulating through the venue that Leo Fender had died, and upon hearing such news, some dealers raised the prices on the "pre-CBS" Fender instruments they were offering for sale. This probably struck some guitar lovers as ironic, since the legendary builder/inventor hadn't been associated with the company that bears his name since 1965, although Leo Fender continued to design and build instruments until his death. The day before he died, he worked on a prototype six-string bass guitar.

Leo Fender's sale agreement included a consultant designation with CBS/Fender that frustrated him, so in the middle of the '70s, a new brand of instruments made at Mr. Fender's CLF Research company in Fullerton premiered. Music Man guitars and basses were marketed by some of Mr. Fender's former business associates, but the venture proved to be short-lived. "Leo era" Music Man instruments were only made for a few years, and while they were well-built, they weren't as revolutionary in the fretted instrument market as original Fender models were in their time.

Original Music Man guitars and basses consisted of two series, Sting Rays and Sabres. Interestingly, the silhouettes of those instruments' bodies were introduced in reverse order, compared to earlier Fender solidbodies—the Sting Ray was the Music Man's initial offering, and had a Jazzmaster-like offset body, while the Sabre, debuting in 1978, had a parallel-waist body, like a Stratocaster.

The most respected and desirable "Leo era" Music Man instrument is the Sting Ray bass—it's a favorite of many "funk"-oriented players and has a distinctive "3 + 1" headstock (but wasn't the first bass to have such). The 1978 Sabre I guitar shown here is well-made, but looks somewhat generic, doesn't it?

By 1980, Mr. Fender was making and marketing the last brand he would be associated with, G & L (in the mid-'80s, the Music Man name and designs would be acquired by the Ernie Ball company, located in San Luis Obispo). G & L guitars and basses would gain a nominal amount of acceptance in the market, and one reason was Mr. Fender's ultimate decision that some G & L instruments would be refined versions of guitars and basses designed when he owned the Fender company.

Some unique "Leo-era" G & L instruments (guitars and basses made prior to Mr. Fender's death) were also created. The company's first guitar was the F-100, and comparing this first-year model (with a nicely-figured ash body) to the Music Man Sabre avers that they're practically the same instrument.

F-100, 1980.
$500

L-1000, 1980. $600

The L-1000 was G & L's first bass, and the one shown here is also a first-year model. This *particular* L-1000 is also unique in that it's N.O.S. It was placed on layaway at a music store in 1981, apparently forgotten by customer and retailer, and was placed back out for sale at the store in 1997 (and was immediately pounced on by a collector). Not surprisingly, it's in dead mint condition.

This 1982 G-200 is quite rare, even for a Leo-era G & L. It's the only G & L that has a Gibson-like scale (24¾ inches) and a control layout like a Les Paul. Most of the approximately 200 examples of G & L's second guitar model had their controls installed on the top of the body in a "cloud"-shaped plate, but it is estimated that the last 12 to 20 G-200s made had their controls installed through the rear of the body (again, like a Gibson Les Paul), and that's the case for this guitar. It, too, is in mint condition.

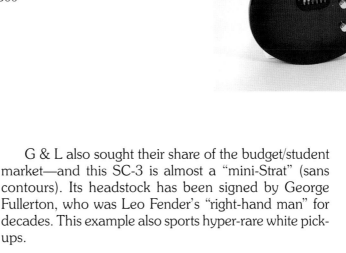

G-200, 1982
$650

SC-3, 1983.
$500

G & L also sought their share of the budget/student market—and this SC-3 is almost a "mini-Strat" (sans contours). Its headstock has been signed by George Fullerton, who was Leo Fender's "right-hand man" for decades. This example also sports hyper-rare white pick-ups.

Interceptor, 1984.
$600

The Interceptor went through more than one body style, and this 1984 example was the most "non-traditional." It's almost X-shaped, and the unusual forearm "scoop" (in lieu of a bevel) is actually more comfortable than it looks. The gold hardware on this particular guitar is also a plus. Interceptors were also quite rare, perhaps for aesthetic reasons.

LIMITED EDITIONS AND CUSTOM-MADE INSTRUMENTS

The guitars and basses that belong to the groups noted in the title of this chapter are, by their very designation, unique in the fretted electric instrument market (new, used, *and* vintage). However, "limited edition" doesn't necessarily mean "future collectible" (which is why the 1985 Gibson XPL "Custom Shop Edition" was placed in another chapter), nor does "limited edition" necessarily mean "rare" (as we'll soon see). Moreover, a custom-made, one-of-a-kind instrument may be the ultimate in "rarity," but some cynics might think it means the ultimate in egotism as well. Nevertheless, such guitars and basses will normally generate a bit of extra interest to most fretted instrument aficionados, and manufacturers have gotten increasingly oriented towards such segments of the guitar market throughout the decades.

California's Alembic company claims to have been the first guitar maker to place active circuitry in instruments, beginning in 1969. Known initially for their association with such San Francisco-area bands as the Grateful Dead, Alembic's guitars and basses were all custom-made for many years before the company entered into standardized production of some models. Alembic instruments are known for innovative circuitry and exotic construction, and this 1982 Distillate DMSB bass is a definitive example. It's constructed of six hardwoods—its five-piece laminated through-the-body neck is made of maple and purpleheart, its fretboard is ebony, its headstock veneers are koa, and its body is mahogany, with a gorgeous Hawaiian flame koa top. It has active circuitry, of course, and its custom features (in addition to the woods selected) include a deeper treble cutaway and a 1/8-inch wider neck.

Alembic Distillate DMSB, 1982. Custom made, $?

Veteran Left Coast luthier R.C. Allen has been hand-crafting instruments since the '50s, and like many solitary builders with small shops, most of his instruments are custom-made. Here's one of his most unique creations, obviously made for a Green Bay Packers fan. Note the "G" logo on the headstock and the 12th fret, the thumbprint inlay that reverses to the treble side after the 12th fret, and the checkered body binding. The pickups on this guitar were personally wound by guitar electronics mogul Seymour Duncan.

R.C. Allen "PackerPicker,"
1996. Custom made, $?

Chandler Austin
Special, 1994.
Custom made, $?

Another California company that has made some inroads into the guitar market is Chandler. Starting out by specializing in accessories—pickguards in particular—Adrian and Paul Chandler and their associates have marketed some unique guitars and basses as well. This "Austin Special" was custom-ordered with an extra "lipstick tube" pickup (total of four), special wiring, a maple fretboard, and tortoise-shell trim, all of which give it a distinct retro-vibe, sonically and visually.

One of Fender's first "limited edition" series was the 25th Anniversary Stratocaster, and its total production was around 10,000 instruments (pretty robust for a model that was marketed as something implicitly rare). Each example has a unique serial number on the neckplate, and an "ANNIVERSARY" designation on the upper body. The first 500 or so were a very pale silver (almost white), but paint problems forced Fender to switch to a different color that was inspired by a silver Porsche finish. It's also intriguing that this model had *four-bolt* neck attachment construction, while at the same time, standard Strats had the notorious three-bolt system. Bill Carson's autograph is unique to this example (he signed it in 1991).

Fender Stratocaster 25th Anniversary Limited Edition, 1979. $1000

Gibson Explorer, 1976. $1000

Here's a 1976 Gibson Explorer with the term "limited edition" included on its small, oval-shaped serial number sticker, but it appears that the production of these guitars went on for quite some time. They weren't true re-issues of the original (and rare) late-'50s Explorers—the progenitors were made of African limba wood (marketed as "korina"), while the mid-'70s models had mahogany bodies. Nevertheless, the '70s Explorers represented Gibson's first attempt at re-introducing their bizarre, zig-zag instrument (which is surprisingly comfortable).

152

The 1971 Sam Ash SG-100 may be rare (at the most, reported a longtime company associate, 250 were made), but it's not particularly impressive. It's based on the "regular" SG-100 (part of the series that replaced Melody Maker), but it has a Gibson humbucking pickup instead of the usual single-coil unit, and its cherry sunburst finish is also unique. The Sam Ash musical instrument retail chain may have bought enough instruments to merit an exclusive for the entire country, but this is still a chunky, uninspiring '70s budget model from Gibson.

Kramer DMZ-6000G, 1979. $450

Gibson Sam Ash SG-100, 1971. $300

In 1979, Kramer's DMZ-6000G was advertised as part of a "limited production series." It still had an aluminum neck with "tuning fork" headstock, but note the "crown" inlays, and an attractive body of laminated American black burl walnut and birds-eye maple. It also featured "DBL" active circuitry.

Obviously, the Metropolitan Tanglewood seen here was inspired by the old Valco "map" guitars of the early '60s, but the construction and sound of these Texas-made instruments are vastly superior to their visual predecessors. Metropolitan is a division of Alamo Music Products of Houston, a highly underrated manufacturer with a unique history in the annals of guitar-making (see next chapter). This Tanglewood is, as of this writing, the only natural-finished example that's ever been made ("It took a long time to find a decent piece of swamp ash," says Alamo President David Wintz). Other custom aesthetics include fret inlay that "crosses over" to the treble side after the 12th fret, as well as the tortoise-shell pickguard headstock overlay (shades of the Harmony H-76!). Again, the pickups on this guitar were personally wound by Seymour Duncan.

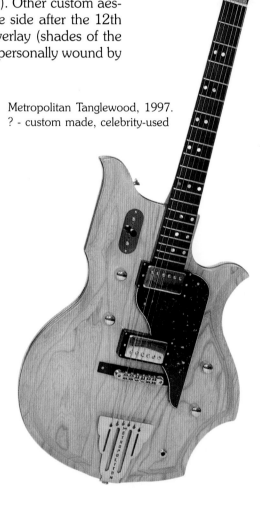

Metropolitan Tanglewood, 1997.
? - custom made, celebrity-used

Rhyne, 1975. ? - cusstom made, celebrity used

Jeff Carlisi's custom-made Explorer-shaped guitar, crafted by Georgia luthier Jay Rhyne in 1975, epitomizes the propriatery importance of such instruments to professional musicians—it's been Carlisi's primary stage guitar ever since he got it. Its body was traced from an original late '50s Explorer owned by Lynyrd Skynyrd guitarist Allen Collins (now deceased), and it also has such aesthetic niceties as "bird"-shaped fretboard inlay and a rosewood pickguard. It's rocked out on stages all over the world, and has held up fine, according to Carlisi, so it should merit a moderate amount of respect from guitar lovers.

Last but not least, there's the Robin Wedge, also from the same company that begat the Metropolitan Tanglewood (Robin is Alamo's flagship brand). It's the only U.S.-made *Wedge* ever constructed, but it's not the *only* Robin Wedge ever constructed (details upcoming). It's part of a trio of instruments made for a retailer—the other two were shaped like a Flying V and an Explorer, but this guitar has its own distinct silhouette; i.e. Gibson never made anything that looked like this. Like an Explorer, this *Wedge* is balanced and comfortable, even though the body shape may imply awkward ergonomics. And like the original '50s Explorers and Flying Vs, the trio of Robin instruments built for the retailer are made from African limba/"korina." So this *Wedge* literally is an American-made, one-of-a-kind instrument.

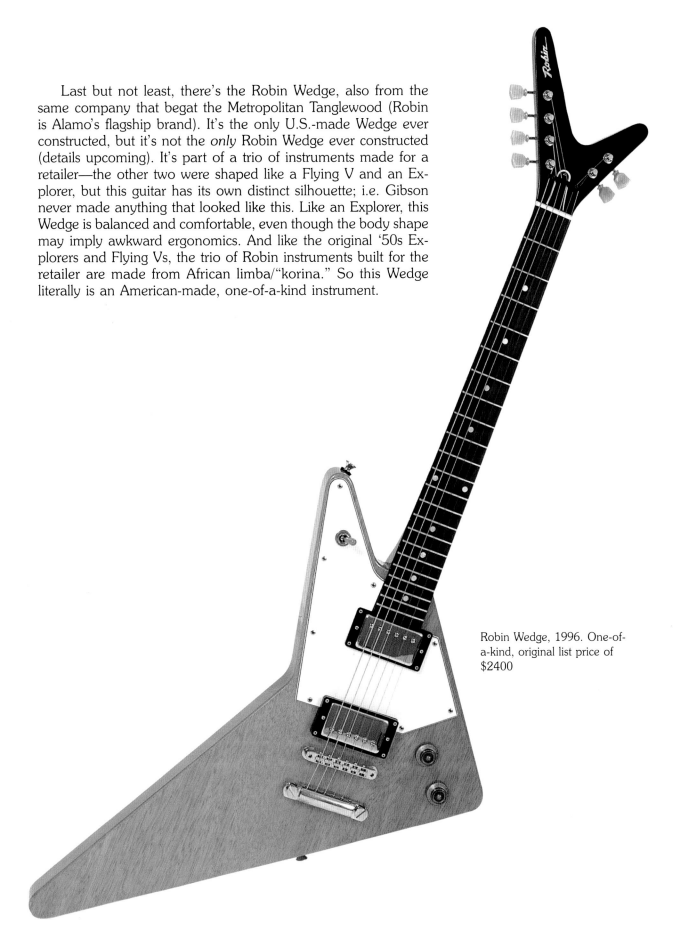

Robin Wedge, 1996. One-of-a-kind, original list price of $2400

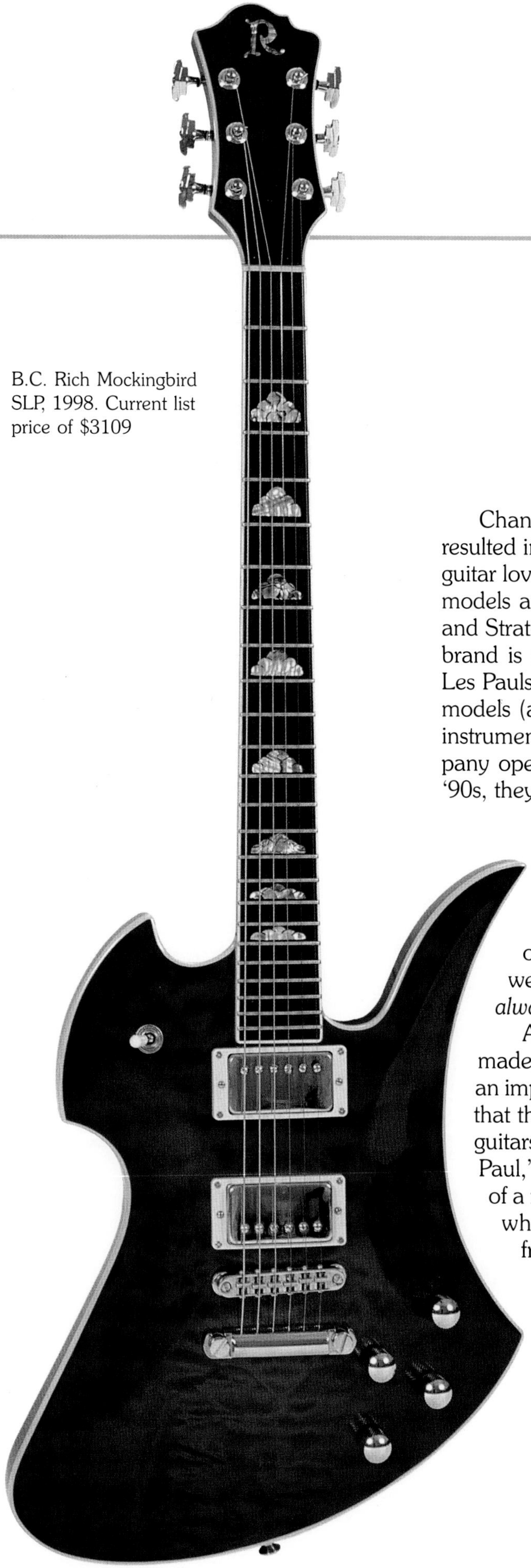

B.C. Rich Mockingbird
SLP, 1998. Current list
price of $3109

Changes in ownership for Fender and Gibson in the mid-'80s resulted in a return to top-of-the-pyramid status in the eyes of many guitar lovers by the end of the century, and the companies' frontline models are based on original '50s styles (single-cutaway Les Pauls and Stratocasters lead the pack). However, Gibson's Epiphone sub-brand is still made almost exclusively overseas, and now includes Les Pauls, SGs, and other models that used to be exclusive Gibson models (and that used to be made exclusively in the U.S.). Fender instruments have been made in several countries, and while the company opened a huge new facility in Corona, California in the late '90s, they've also developed an even-larger *maquilladora* factory in Ensenada, B.C., Mexico, and there's a lot of interdependence between the California and Mexican operations.

However, Bill Carson's perspective on the Mexican operation is interesting, as he referred to the company's primeval times in Fullerton in the '50s: "The vast majority of Fender's workers during the earliest days of the company were Mexican, so as far as I'm concerned, Mexicans have *always* built Fender guitars."

At the turn of the century, B.C. Rich was offering American-made instruments on a very limited basis; i.e., it's still primarily an imported line. However, the Mockingbird SLP seen here avers that the brand is still offering some gorgeous yet hyper-rare U.S. guitars. The "SLP" designation apparently stands for "Slash Les Paul," as it has Les Paul-type construction (with the exception of a neck-through configuration), and was designed for the erstwhile guitarist for Guns 'n Roses. The beautiful "cloud" fretboard inlay is abalone pearl.

Remarkably, some relatively new U.S. manufacturers managed to thrive during a time when other once-mighty American brands names were relegated to the headstocks of imported instruments. Illinois' Hamer company began to garner attention in the mid-'70s, and a lot of their high-quality instruments had some distinct retro-vibe facets. Note the figured maple, vintage-style sunburst finish, and late '50s Les Paul Special/Jr. silhouette on this 1980 Special. Hamer was ultimately acquired by Kaman Music (owners of Ovation), and is still offering very underrated instruments.

Hamer Special, 1980.
$450

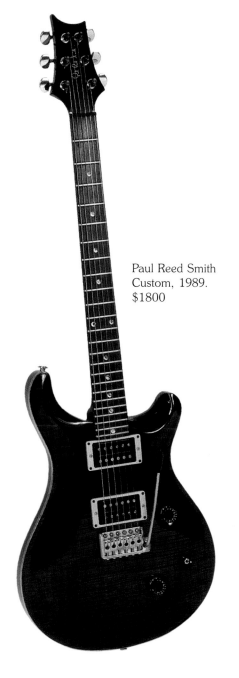

Paul Reed Smith
Custom, 1989.
$1800

Paul Reed Smith is a modern American success story. The Maryland manufacturer came to prominence in the mid-'80s, and has been making exquisite and acclaimed instruments at a time when other companies have stumbled or seen their brand names end up primarily on imported models (B.C. Rich and Dean come to mind). On some PRS special editions, there's been a waiting list that includes notable rock stars.

Joe Naylor's Reverend instruments are relatively new in the marketplace (introduced in 1996), and have obvious Danelectro-inspired aesthetics, but construction-wise, they're even more unique: The front and back are a wood-based phenolic product, somewhat akin to Masonite, but the company orders a specific thickness of the material to facilitate optimum resonance. Moreover, the bodies of Reverend guitars and basses have a mahogany center block which improves both the balance *and* sound, so this line, which is available in all sorts of neo-retro colors such as "'57 Turquoise," epitomizes the "back to the future" line of thinking for some modern manufacturers.

No current U.S. manufacturer probably has a more intriguing production history than Houston's Alamo Music Products. A noted Houston retailer, Rockin' Robin, began importing guitars bearing the Robin moniker in the early '80s, and in the latter part of that decade, builder/designer/Rockin' Robin associate David Wintz opted to switch to *domestic* guitar production, in a reverse move when compared to what other U.S. brands were doing. Wintz's company now makes three brands—Robin, Metropolitan, and Alamo—and all three brands have a distinct amount of retro-cool in their styling. In some cases, such as the Robin Wedge, there were imported versions of the style but no domestic production (the U.S.-made Wedge in the previous chapter is one-of-a-kind), and the Alamo guitars made by Wintz and associates are quite different from the ones cited in the "One-Shots" chapter. The '97 Robin Freedom bass seen here had an imported progenitor, and this example is, according to Wintz, one of the earliest U.S.-made Freedom basses. It may date from the latter '90s, but it reeks of good ol' vintage panache, and it sounds and plays a lot better than most of '50s predecessors it resembles.

Hamer, Paul Reed Smith, Reverend and Robin (as well as other Alamo Music brands) exemplify the notion that even though the days of dominance for American guitar manufacturers are probably gone forever, the *quality* of today's U. S.-made instruments may be an acceptable alternative to the lack of *quantity* to anyone with a legitimate interest in electric guitars and basses as collectible pieces of Americana. Also, as noted earlier, there's that incessant "time warp" appeal to oh-so-many Boomers.

It helps to whet one's appetite for such icons by realizing that the instruments seen in this book are only a small portion of the fascinating fretted items that were created in the United States in the second half of the 20th century. There are an untold number of other brands and models that can (and should) be sought out, cleaned up, and given the respect they deserve.

In other words, you've just seen the tip of the proverbial iceberg.

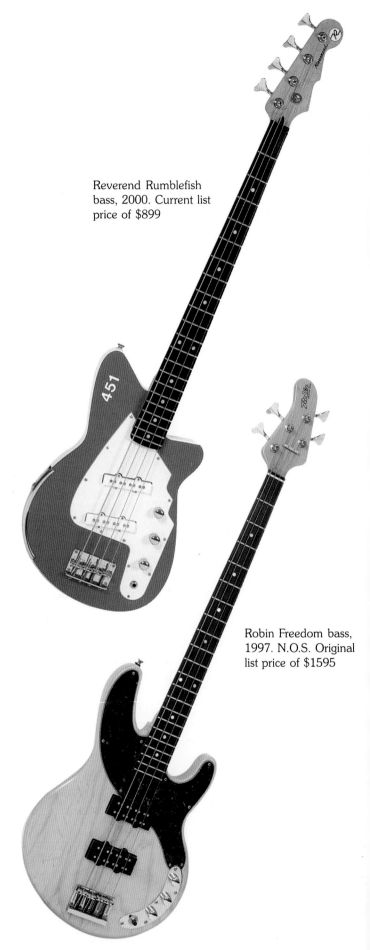

Reverend Rumblefish bass, 2000. Current list price of $899

Robin Freedom bass, 1997. N.O.S. Original list price of $1595

BIBLIOGRAPHY

In addition to the extensive catalogue research (including contributions from several individuals), the following books were sources for the preparation of the text in *Vintage Electric Guitars: In Praise of Fretted Americana.*

Bacon, Tony & Day, Paul. *The Gibson Les Paul Book* (San Francisco, California: Miller Freeman Books, 1994)

Bacon, Tony & Moorhouse, Barry. *The Bass Book* (San Francisco, California: Miller Freeman Books, 1995)

Bechtoldt, Paul. *G & L: Leo's Legacy* (Peckville, Pennsylvania: Woof Associates, 1994)

Bechtoldt, Paul. *Guitars From Neptune* (Peckville, Pennsylvania: Backporch, 1995)

Bulli, John. *Guitar History, Volume I: Gibson SG* (Westport, Connecticut: The Bold Strummer, Ltd., 1999

Carson, Bill & Moseley, Willie. *Bill Carson: My Life and Times with Fender Musical Instruments* (Bismarck, North Dakota: Vintage Guitar Books, 1998)

Carter, Walter. *Gibson Guitars: 100 Years of an American Icon* (Los Angeles, California: General Publishing Group, Inc., 1994)

Carter, Walter. *Epiphone: The Complete History* (Milwaukee, Wisconsin: Hal Leonard Corporation, 1995)

Carter, Walter. *The Martin Book* (San Francisco, California: Miller Freeman Books, 1995)

Carter, Walter. *The History of the Ovation Guitar* (Milwaukee, Wisconsin: Hal Leonard Corporation, 1996)

Duchossoir, A.R. *Guitar Identification: Fender-Gibson-Gretsch-Martin* (Milwaukee, Wisconsin: Hal Leonard Corporation, 1983)

Duchossoir, A.R. *Gibson Electrics: The Classic Years* (Milwaukee, Wisconsin: Hal Leonard Corporation, 1994)

Duchossoir, A.R. *The Fender Telecaster* (Milwaukee, Wisconsin: Hal Leonard Corporation, 1991)

Fisch, Jim & Fred, L.B. *Epiphone: The House of Stathopoulo* (New York, New York: Amsco Publications, 1996)

Greenwood, Alan, & Hembree, Gil. *The Official Vintage Guitar Magazine Price Guide.* (Bismark, North Dakota: Vintage Guitar Books, 2000)

Gruhn, George & Carter, Walter. *Electric Guitars and Basses: A Photographic History* (San Francisco: Miller Freeman Books, 1994)

Gruhn, George & Carter, Walter. *Gruhn's Guide to Vintage Guitars* (second edition) (San Francisco: Miller Freeman Books, 1999)

Hopkins, Gregg & Moore, Bill. *Ampeg: The Story Behind the Sound* (Milwaukee, Wisconsin: Hal Leonard Corporation, 1999)

Moseley, Willie. *Classic Guitars U.S.A.* (Fullerton, California: Centerstream Publishing, 1992)

Moseley, Willie. *Stellas & Stratocasters* (Bismarck, North Dakota: Vintage Guitar Books, 1994)

Moseley, Willie. *Guitar People* (Bismarck, North Dakota: Vintage Guitar Books, 1998)

Moust, Hans. *The Guild Guitar Book* (Breda; the Netherlands: GuitArchives Publications, 1995)

Scott, Jay. Gretsch: *The Guitars of the Fred Gretsch Company* (Fullerton, California: Centerstream Publishing, 1992)

Scott, Jay. *'50s Cool: Kay Guitars* (Hauppauge, New York: Seventh String Press, 1992)

Smith, Richard. *The History of Rickenbacker Guitars* (Fullerton, California: Centerstream Publishing, 1987)

Smith, Richard. *Fender: The Sound Heard 'Round the World* (Fullerton, California: Garfish Publishing Co., 1995)

Wheeler, Tom. *American Guitars* (revised and updated edition) (New York, New York: HarperCollins Publishers, 1992)

Wright, Michael. *Guitar Stories, Vol. 1* (Bismarck, North Dakota: Vintage Guitar Books, 1995)

Wright, Michael. *Guitar Stories, Vol. 2* (Bismarck, North Dakota: Vintage Guitar Books, 2000)